FOLK ART AND AGING

MATERIAL
VERNACULARS

Jason Baird Jackson, *editor*

FOLK ART AND AGING
Life-Story Objects and Their Makers

Jon Kay

Indiana University Press, in cooperation with the

Mathers Museum of World Cultures, Indiana University

Bloomington and Indianapolis

This book is a publication of

Indiana University Press
Office of Scholarly Publishing
Herman B Wells Library 350
1320 East 10th Street
Bloomington, Indiana 47405 USA

iupress.indiana.edu

Manufactured in the United States of America

Library of Congress Cataloging-in-Publication Data

Names: Kay, Jon, author.
Title: Folk art and aging : life-story objects and their makers /
    Jon Kay.
Description: Bloomington : Indiana University Press, [2016] |
    Series: Material vernaculars | Includes bibliographical references
    and index.
Identifiers: LCCN 2016017119| ISBN 9780253022066 (cloth :
    alk. paper) | ISBN 9780253022165 (pbk. : alk. paper) |
    ISBN 9780253022202 (ebook)
Subjects: LCSH: Folk art—Psychological aspects. | Art therapy for
    older people. | Memory in art. | Aging—Psychological aspects. |
    Folk artists—United States—Biography.
Classification: LCC N5312 .K39 2016 | DDC 745.01/9—dc23
LC record available at https://lccn.loc.gov/2016017119

1 2 3 4 5   21 20 19 18 17 16

For Bob, Gus, John, Marian, and Milan
May your stories be remembered and your art treasured

Contents

List of Illustrations

Acknowledgments

I<small>N THE</small> 1970s, just before my grandfather retired from the *Pekin Banner* in Washington County, Indiana, the paper switched from a movable-type system to a newer method; so my grandfather brought home the drawers that once organized the metal letters and hung a few of these ready-made shadow boxes on the walls. He filled the divided drawers with old pocketknives, arrowheads, marbles, and a variety of other keepsakes from his life. He used these objects to launch into stories about his youth and life in southern Indiana. I credit my grandfather, Harry Axsom, for sparking my interest in the narrative nature of things and starting me on my life's work of listening to the stories of elders and learning from the things they make, display, and share.

The insights that led to this book are the product of years of working with elderly storytellers, tradition bearers, and artists too numerous to name, but I am thankful for their patience with me and for the many lessons they taught me. Three elders whom I will name are Damon Helton, a willow furniture maker from Middlesboro, Kentucky; Zelton Connor, a storyteller from the Okefenokee Swamp; and Nancy Morgan, a quilter in White Springs, Florida. Each of you taught me the true importance of the arts in later life and how the stories and skills we learn in our youth can help us as we age.

From Warren Roberts and Michael Ann Williams, to Richard Bauman and Henry Glassie, many teachers have shaped my research perspectives and understanding of folklore and folk art. I thank them all. I am grateful as well for the thoughtful advice and support of my friends and colleagues in the Department of Folklore and Ethnomusicology at Indiana University, but especially for Pravina Shukla, Diane Goldstein, and Michael Dylan Foster, who offered comments on this manuscript and whose collective depth and breadth of knowledge made this book better. Jason Baird Jackson, my friend and teacher, deserves special credit, for without him this book would not exist. I also thank two reviewers, Marsha MacDowell and Daniel Swan, whose valuable comments improved this work.

I would be remiss if I did not recognize the graduate assistants and workers at Traditional Arts Indiana, who contributed greatly to my research, work, and knowledge. I appreciate each of you: Ilze Akerbergs, Jill Hemming Austin, Arle Lommel, Christopher Mulé, Maria Kennedy, Selina Morales, Kat Forgacs, Thomas Grant Richardson, Hsinwen Hsu, Joseph O'Connell, Jennifer Jameson, Kate Schramm, Suzanne Godby Ingalsbe, Anna Mulé, Kara Bayless,

Josephine McRobbie, Betsy Shepherd, Kelley Totten, Hannah Davis, Meghan Smith, Emily Polembella, Meredith McGriff, and Maria Zeringue.

Finally, I thank my parents, Emil and Marilyn Kay, and my in-laws, Johnny and Sharon Dorn, for their support in my work and my life. However, I truly could not have written this book without the support and sacrifice of my wife, Mandy, and my son, Zelton—I love you both very much.

FOLK ART AND AGING

Introduction: Folk Art and Aging

> There are elderly people all over America, waiting only to be asked about their stories and folk art. Their memories and works are stored in boxes, in cellars, in trunks, in attics . . . needing only a witness to bring them to light, a recipient to complete the interchange that is requisite to all cultural transmission.
>
> (Myerhoff 1984a:38)

I ARRIVE AT THE Indiana State Fairgrounds on a hot July afternoon to interview Harold Stark, a longtime state fair volunteer, and steam engine enthusiast. It is still weeks until the fair, but the eighty-nine-year-old senior is busy moving tractors and equipment into place for the big event. The fair selected Harold as this year's Indiana State Fair Master, an award that the program I direct (Traditional Arts Indiana) produces for the fair. From sheep shearers to fiddlers, I have produced short documentaries about the fair's veteran competitors, judges, and performers for this program. Like several of the other State Fair Masters, Harold is dedicated, gregarious, and elderly. At nearly ninety, the retired mechanical engineer and machinist continues to work throughout the year repairing the old farm implements that the fair's pioneer village uses in its historical demonstrations. He explains, "If it's broken, I can take it home and weld it or maybe make a new piece." In providing this and other services, the volunteer remains an important knowledge bearer and worker for the village, despite his advanced years.

Harold's association with the fair began when he started exhibiting the half-size steam engine that he built. He completed his homemade machine in 1976 shortly before retiring (figure 0.1). For decades, Harold has driven his small engine in tractor-show parades, used it to power buzz saws, and plough fields, but more importantly, it helps him to connect socially with others, teach about Indiana's agricultural and industrial heritage, and share his personal story about helping his grandfather on the family farm. Harold built the engine to commemorate his family's tradition of working with steam and to recall his grandfather's influence. He explains:

> Well, my grandfather (my mother's father) raised his family on an eighty-acre farm down in Rush County and the farm only had about fifty acres of it tillable. The rest of it was Little Blue River running right through the middle of it. And he had a large steam engine, a saw mill, a big separator, clover hauler, and then he would help (back in probably before World War I) use that big engine and

Fig. 0.1 Harold Stark's half-size steam engine, 2012.

helped pull the road grader. (He said several times, where they helped build three-mile stretches of county road back then). And I got involved with helping him when I was nine years old, polishing all the brass. And then when I got a little older, he'd take us on Sunday to drain the engine and do a boiler wash, so he got all the sediment and the dirt out of the boiler so it wouldn't destroy it. And I learned, started in at that age and then studied it.

And then the equipment that he owned when he died in late '34—the equipment all got sold to settle his estate and I never got to run any of it, because I was so small. They said at that time I wasn't "dry enough behind the ears to do any of that stuff." But I built this engine... I built it as a memorial to my grandfather and all of my uncles.

Although Harold built his engine to remember the past, he uses it today at the fair and other events to share stories and communicate his values to younger generations. He notes that the pioneer village aims to show fairgoers "where this country has advanced and progressed from—hard manual labor prior to World War I or after the Civil War, all the way up through the Industrial Revolution to what we have today." He stresses that "what the kids today are enjoying [are the] by-products of the space age."[1] Though his half-size steam engine has brought him years of enjoyment and personal reminiscence, it also serves as a useful tool for teaching children about Indiana's agricultural past and telling others about his childhood experiences.[2]

Just as it does the work of tilling a field, Harold's engine has helped the senior develop a post-retirement identity as a steam engineer; and through his demonstrations at various antique tractor shows and fairs, he continues to use the engine to connect socially with others. His newfound role as a teacher, demonstrator, and repairman keeps him busy, which is one of the primary reasons he built his engine. He reflects:

> I told the people when I retired from Allison that I wasn't gonna be like the average retiree, get myself in a rocking chair and sit on the front porch and watch the cars go by as they went down in front of the house on Meridian Street. I said, "I'm going to keep busy!" I have done that.

Between his work with the pioneer village, going to antique tractor shows, and helping his friends and family, Harold has had very little "TV and rocking-chair time" since his retirement.

Elders like Harold make, use, and/or display objects to recall, reflect upon, and share their lives. In this book I explore how older adults use folk art, specifically material forms of life stories, as a strategy for coping with some of the difficulties they face as they age. Often deployed to express their personal or cultural identities, these distinctive objects also help maintain and forge connections with family and friends, and assist in distilling and telling their own meaningful life stories.

Although some people make art throughout their lives, many gerontologists recognize that old age is often the creative age. Geriatric psychiatrist Gene Cohen calls attention to studies on "psychological growth and development in the second half of life," which have brought about a greater appreciation of the impact that creative activity and artmaking have on a senior's ability to enact "positive change" in their lives (Cohen 2006:8). He goes on to note that unlike other genres of art where the elderly may be the exception, elders play a prominent role in creating and maintaining many folk arts. He writes:

> Often when older people are recognized for outstanding work, they are typically regarded as exceptions to the rule—as if creativity and outstanding performance were not significant parts of aging. But when you can identify an entire field like folk art that is dominated by older people, then outstanding performance by various older individuals cannot be trivialized as atypical or an exception to the rule. Folk art makes a profoundly powerful statement about the inherent capacity for creative expression throughout the entire life cycle. (2006:8)

Why do some elders continue, take up, or revive a folk art? Why do others focus their energy on a meaningful craft or creative practice? Through close study, I believe there are important lessons to be learned from the folk art practices of older adults.

Fig. 0.2 John Bontrager knotting a rug at the Center for the Traditional Arts in Shipshewana, Indiana, 2009.

John Bontrager, an Amish rag-rug maker, began weaving after he retired from farming and his wife passed away. This home craft provides the widower with a small source of income, but more importantly, it is a vital time-filling activity for the lonely senior. John enjoys demonstrating at the Center for the Traditional Arts, an arts cooperative that promotes traditional crafts in Shipshewana, Indiana. While he knots the fringe of his rugs at the center, he visits with other area artisans and talks with the public (figure 0.2). Making rugs offers utility in the elder's life far beyond the mere production of floor coverings and making money—it provides the weaver with a sense of personal mastery and serves as a tool for social engagement (Cohen 2006:11).

Comparably, Eli Jackson, a retired machinist and minister from Muncie, Indiana, developed a second career making banjos and dulcimers, a craft revived from his youth in Kentucky, where he grew up around music and instrument making. Through building simple one-string instruments he called "canjoes," Eli taught hundreds of children about music, Appalachian culture, and his personal story of growing up during the Great Depression. He recalled swiping wire from his mother's screen door when he was young in order to make similar instruments. In retirement, the senior busied himself doing hands-on programs at area schools, festivals, and museums (figure 0.3).[3]

The work of both Eli and John shows a range of instrumental and expressive uses of art and artmaking in the lives of seniors. While their crafts are important

Fig. 0.3 Eli Jackson at Conner Prairie playing a mandolin made from a ham can, 2007.

to each of the artisans, the instrument maker's hobby provides the additional benefit of being a tool for sharing his life story, and the rug maker uses his craft to keep busy and feel productive in a community where work and industriousness are highly valued. In the chapters to come, I look at these diverse uses of artmaking in the lives of older adults, focusing specifically on the connection between life review, personal experience narratives, and the material objects that elders make.

The combined processes of seniors reviewing their lives, making art based upon this reflection, and narrating their creations for others is a distinctive and widespread phenomenon that deserves more attention.[4] For some, quilts, woodcarvings, or paintings become vehicles for sharing important and useful life stories. Whereas elders such as Harold may create one special object to remember and share their past, others like Eli produce many works, to assist with their life review and narrative undertakings. Joe Casey, an African American self-taught artist in South Bend, Indiana, painted scenes from his youth growing up in Missouri. When he passed away in 1999, dozens of paintings filled his home that visually recalled his life. Barbara Kirshenblatt-Gimblett aptly termed artifacts such as Joe's paintings, Eli's instruments, and Harold's engine as "memory objects." She writes:

Some individuals create *memory objects* as a way to materialize internal images, and through them, to recapture earlier experiences. Whereas souvenirs are saved prospectively, with a sense of their future ability to call back memories, memory objects are produced retrospectively, long after the events they depict transpired. (1985:331)

She also observes that these creations can act as tools for reviewing and sharing personal stories, and provide a catalyst for conversations and social interactions (336).

Such "life-story objects" are those material items that elders keep, display, and arrange that relate to and help communicate one's personal memories and stories. Souvenirs and private possessions can be used to recall experiences, linking the past with present situations. As noted above, though, a specific subset of life-story objects goes beyond persistent, personal, possessions and are works specifically crafted to assist in the structuring and telling of life experiences. Some older adults use these works to elicit interest, explicate personal narratives, and share personal beliefs and values. Whether artfully arranging family photographs, painting pictures of past events, or woodburning important names and places onto a walking stick, life-story objects often anticipate social interactions and storytelling events, which is just one aspect of their creative utility and complex role in the lives of elders. To reduce memory paintings, story quilts, and other forms of life-story objects to mere works of art or storytelling props fails to appreciate the complex and diverse narrative nature of these creations and the process that brought them into existence. The making and use of these objects serves multiple functions in the lives of seniors: they are objects to reflect upon; props for explaining events and their meanings; the product of a pastime that fills the lonely hours; mnemonic devices to remind the forgetful; a meditative practice that helps seniors make sense of the past; and a material legacy to leave to family and friends.

We will come to understand some of the various uses of these dynamic expressive forms through the work of five elders living in Indiana: Bob Taylor, a retired patternmaker and memory carver; Gustav Potthoff, a painter and survivor of the death camps of Burma and Thailand; Marian Sykes, a rug maker and retired working-mother from Chicago; John Schoolman, a prolific walking stick maker and hiker; and Milan Opacich, a Serbian-American instrument maker and storyteller. As part of my work as the director of Traditional Arts Indiana, I came to know each of these artists, whose distinctive memory projects piqued my interest. Bob, Gus, John, Marian, and Milan show us the ways in which elders contemplate, make, display, and narrate their life-story objects. They also help us grasp how their creative work assists them in making sense of their lives, connecting with others, forging a new identity in their later years, and making commentary of the modern world around them.

On the surface, the artists featured here may seem to have little in common other than they are all over eighty years old and live in Indiana. Four are men and one is a woman. They represent a range of ethnic backgrounds: Serbian, Dutch-Indonesian, Sicilian, and just plain Hoosier. However, by focusing specifically on their narrative and artmaking projects, other similarities become apparent: many have stories of trauma or loss; retirement marked a special flowering of their creative drive; their artistic work became more than a pastime and provided them with a new identity; and the objects they make encourage the telling of positive life stories.

Notes

1. Harold is not alone in his use of antique tractors and farm implements to comment on the contemporary world: several seniors who grew up on farms have returned to restoring and displaying iconic farm equipment to recall the past and comment on contemporary life (Cashman 2006).

2. Simon Bronner similarly observes that senior carvers make wooden chains and other items to demonstrate "their knowledge to younger generations," in the hopes that they "will be remembered after death as practitioners of a custom that represents traditional, often rural values" (Bronner 1996:129). Folk crafts and life-story objects are often links between past and future generations, where the maker stands as a witness to earlier events and practices of people (Myerhoff 1984a:38).

3. I worked with Eli Jackson to do several programs around the state before his death in 2009. He demonstrated at the Minnetrista Cultural Center in Muncie, Indiana, and did workshops and demonstrations at Conner Prairie in Fishers, Indiana, as part of a special program on Indiana instrument builders.

4. Scholars working in the 1980s brought the study of material life-review into academic discourse (Babcock 1986; Beck 1988; Bronner 1996; Bustin and Kane 1982; Erhard 1983; Ferris 1982; Hufford 1984; Hufford, Hunt, and Zeitlin 1987; Kirshenblatt-Gimblett 1985; Mullen 1992; Myerhoff 1986). In recent years, as Simon Bronner recently noted, fewer scholars have published on this front (Bronner 2015). A noteworthy exception is *They Called Me Mayer July: Painted Memories of a Jewish Childhood in Poland before the Holocaust* (2007), which focuses on the memory paintings of Mayer Kirshenblatt, the father of folklorist and performance-studies scholar Barbara Kirshenblatt-Gimblett. This collaborative work marries the senior's images and stories about the Jewish community in Apt, Poland, with a thoughtful analysis by his daughter, resulting in a very personal and insightful study into life-story art.

1   Bob Taylor: Stories in Wood and Words

Re-membering, then is a purposive, significant, unification, quite different
from the passive continuous fragmentary flickerings of images and feelings
that accompany other activities in the normal flow of consciousness . . . A life
is given shape that extends back in the past and forward into the future. It
becomes a tidy edited tale.

    (Myerhoff 1992:240)

Introduction

In the fall of 2013, the Columbus Area Arts Council invited me to present a workshop on "Folk Art and Aging" at the Mill Race Center, an active-senior facility
that offers a robust range of classes and workshops for area retirees. I agreed,
hoping to solicit feedback on my research and ideas. While going over my presentation at the center before others arrived, a tall, thin man poked his head into the
room. I invited him in and introduced myself. "What do you have there?" I asked,
pointing to the two boards wrapped in towels that he had brought for the show-
and-tell portion of the evening's program. "I do memory carvings," he explained
as he unpacked the boards. On the surface of each, he had carved detailed scenes
from his childhood; the pair of boards visually told the story of a train trip in 1941
that the elder, Bob Taylor, took with his parents to Coney Island in Cincinnati,
Ohio. I was impressed at the artist's mastery of his craft and the narrative details
invested in these panoramic panels.

    "How long have you carved?"

    "Since I was eight years old or so, but didn't start doing the memory carvings
until after I retired."

    My head raced with questions for the carver, but the room was beginning to
fill with more workshop participants. "I want to talk to you more," I said, "but I
have to finish getting ready for the program. Can we talk afterward?"

    Several seniors brought examples of their needlepoint, quilts, woodcarvings,
and other handmade works, which they took turns sharing throughout the evening. Though Bob had brought tabletop stands to display his two carvings, he
placed the boards face down on the table, concealing their beauty. When it came

Fig. 1.1 Bob Taylor in his workshop holding his dead whale carving in Columbus, Indiana. Photograph by Greg Whitaker Photography, 2015.

time for him to share his work, he stood and addressed the room: "Since I have been retired, I've been doing memory carvings of my childhood." Then he lifted the boards and placed them on the stands, revealing the complex carved scenes (figure 1.2). The audience's amazement was audible as they oohed and aahed. He then began to tell the story of his childhood trip to Coney Island and his process of researching and making the panels to commemorate it. "The trip that I brought to show was a trip that we took in 1941 in June," he began. He then outlined the event based in part on his childhood recollections:

> We got on a train in Columbus. We went to Cincinnati; they met us with buses; took us down to the docks. We got on a riverboat and we went to Coney Island, which was about fifteen miles east of Cincinnati.
>
> [Cummins] gave us ride tickets. We packed a lunch, which we ate. I think we ate it on the boat . . . but I was eight and a lot of this was *really* foggy, so I had to go back and do research.

Then he recounted his quest to reclaim the details (and eventually the story) behind his murky childhood memories.

In order to create his scenes, Bob searched for additional information and visual clues about that long-ago trip. He talked with local historians and newspaper columnists, who finally led him to a local woman who had been on the trip

Fig. 1.2 Bob Taylor at the Mill Race Center, Columbus, Indiana, 2013.

and was a few years older. She shared her memories of the day and let him make a copy of a souvenir brochure about the excursion. From his recollections, the brochure, as well as a handful of family photographs from the outing, Bob compiled his set of memory carvings.

The pair of panels tells the two phases of the Coney Island trip. The first shows his family ready to board the train behind the Cummins Building in Columbus. His grandfather, brother, mother, and father are waiting with him, while a brass band plays (figure 1.3). The second panel shows them arriving at Coney Island and includes the Island Queen, the steamboat that ferried them on the river; the Ferris wheel, rollercoaster, swings, and a merry-go-round in the amusement park are shown in the distance (figure 1.4). He even includes a coal barge that his father just happened to snap a picture of that day. The artist's scenes are beautiful compilations of remembered moments and discovered images.

After the presentation, Bob gave me his telephone number, and a week later, I was sitting in his workshop in the basement of his Tipton Lake home in Columbus. He talked about growing up in the midsize town, his lifelong practice of carving, and the personal panels he creates to record childhood memories.

Carver of Memories

As Mary Hufford and other scholars have noted, not all autobiographies "take the form of books," but rather some of the folk-art projects of older adults are "a

Fig. 1.3 Bob Taylor's *Excursion Train to Coney Island* displayed at the Mill Race Center, Columbus, Indiana.

Fig. 1.4 Bob Taylor's Coney Island river trip panel displayed at the Mill Race Center, Columbus, Indiana.

kind of three-dimensional reminiscence for their makers whereby the past bursts into tangible being" (1984:33). But these works are not just "reminiscence" or the recalling of the past, but rather thoughtfully constructed material life-stories. In many ways, Bob Taylor's art is the product of a life of carving and remembering. He blends his gift of storytelling with his love of woodcarving to produce striking narrative scenes about special moments when he was young.

While just a boy, Bob received his first pocketknife from his grandfather. He recalls:

> My grandfather gave me my first pocketknife. It's a red-handled knife. I could get it out of my case there [pointing to his workbench]. Eight years old—I don't know how many people today give their child a knife when they're eight years

old—probably not too many . . . [My grandfather] could see that I was interested. I had already made a little animal or two. So for Christmas one year he gave me a red-handled pocketknife.[1]

Although receiving the red-handled pocketknife started the youth down the path of becoming a woodcarver, his grandfather was not Bob's only carving influence.

Around eleven years old, Bob met legendary carver Mooney Warther.[2] Known for his speed at making wooden pliers and for carving intricate scale models of steam locomotives, Warther set up his traveling woodcarving museum at the Bartholomew County Fair. Bob tells of the carver's demonstration and exhibit that he saw nearly seventy years ago:

We used to go to the fair . . . and just inside the gate, the year that I remember, there was a man. He had a truck and it had a board that let down from the side to make like a stand that he could come out, or a platform where he could come out and talk to the people—a little bit higher than what the people were. And he would come out on the platform with his pocketknife and piece of wood and he would make a few cuts in his piece of wood and make a pair of pliers. And I thought that was cool. I really liked that. I wanted to see him do that again. Well, my folks said, "No, we're going to go look at the 4-H exhibits," which weren't too far from there. And they said, "Okay, well, you just stay right here and we'll pick you up once we come out of the exhibits."

Okay. So I'm waiting for this gentleman to come out again onto the platform. The people that had been in the crowd had gone through the exhibit then and paid a nickel or a dime, whatever it was, to see what was in the truck. And so as they left, a few minutes later he came back out on the platform and saw me standing there. He said, "Can I help you, son?" And I said, "Well, I want to see you do that again." And he said, "Well, would you like to see what's in the truck?" And I said, "I'd love to."

So he came down off the truck, took my hand, led me through the exhibit. And it was the most [unbelievable] things I had ever seen that anybody could do. These were train models that were made out of ebony and ivory and walnut and bone. And so I came back to the front of the exhibit there and met my folks, and of course it worked well because then once I told them what was in the trailer, they had to go, too. And they had to pay the nickel or dime, whatever it was. So, but it was well worth it.

With the knife his grandfather gave him and the inspiration from Warther's traveling museum and show, carving became a passion for the fledgling artist.[3] Bob learned to carve in a variety of styles. As a young Boy Scout, he practiced making neckerchief slides and whittling animals, which helped him develop as a carver.

Once grown, Bob apprenticed as a patternmaker and spent more than twenty years working "on the bench" as a master patternmaker. From engineers' drawings, he carved wooden, three-dimensional prototypes of truck parts, missile components, and many other products. From these patterns, manufacturers produced the molds needed to make metal castings. The last twenty years of his working life, the carver sold patterns internationally for Badger Pattern Works in Milwaukee. However, whether on the bench or off, Bob continued to carve for his own enjoyment.

When his children were young, Bob served as a Boy Scout leader and whittled whimsical neckerchief slides that were even more elaborate than the ones he made when he was young. He remembers, "I always had a sharp tool in my hand doing something, and still do today." Having retired from patternmaking in 1999, he now dedicates much of his carving time to researching and making his memory projects.

Landscape Relief Carving

Bob invests months into researching and designing each memory carving before he ever puts chisel to wood. He enjoys researching the forgotten facts and visual elements that he incorporates into his scenes. An important part of his creative process, the time spent researching locations, people, and events not only informs his designs, but also provides him with additional stories to tell about his panels. As the narrator of his completed carvings, he easily shifts from sharing a childhood memory to talking about uncovering additional information for his scenes.

As I will show throughout this book, elders who make life-story objects often engage in a process of personal discovery and creative expression, frequently followed by a series of presentations or narrations of their creations. Joanne Stuttgen observed:

> By making things, men and women review, reshape and reorder their lives and themselves. The process of manipulating physical materials to reshape disrupted lives is a reversal of ritual, a process in which chaos is inverted and systematically and symbolically arranged. (1992:304)

In Bob's memory carvings, he unites the disparate shards of memories and discovered details into a cohesive recalled world through which he constructs his tight narrative scenes and tells his personal stories.

Once Bob has researched the facts and found period photographs or other relevant visual data, he makes several detailed sketches of his scene. From these illustrations, he compiles a master drawing that renders all of the buildings, cars, trees, and other visual elements to the size they will appear in the completed carving. He tapes this pattern to the top edge of the board to be carved, so that he can easily lift the paper as he works on his relief carving. Using carbon paper, he then traces the complete drawing onto the board and begins to carve. With a gouge and chisels, he removes the traced lines from the wood, first taking away the deepest sections to develop the different depths in the scene. Once he develops these visual levels, he resketches his pattern onto the panel, adding the final elements to his scene. With his chisels, gouges, and mallet, he then painstakingly carves the fine details of his remembered landscape.

Bob's aesthetic aim through this complex process is to make an attractive panel that contains the necessary elements of his story; however, the image must also be as visually accurate as possible. Whether the St. John's Church at White Creek or the Cummins Building in downtown Columbus, each panel evokes the essence of a place so that others can recognize its location. He explains that while the carvings are not "an exact perfect scale model," they do capture "what people remember in their minds."

Although Bob works in a variety of genres, his memory pieces employ a relief style of carving appropriate for landscape scenes. Rupert Kreider (1897–1983), an itinerant carver from Pennsylvania, inspired Bob's approach. Kreider often passed through Bartholomew County, Indiana, where he found work on local farms. Bob never met the carver, but he bought one of his wooden scenes from an antique shop in Hope, Indiana, in 1981. The panel profoundly changed Bob's approach to carving. He recalls:

> It was the inspiration of looking at that piece that gave me the desire to want to figure out how he was doing what he was doing . . . I studied the piece, made some tools, studied some more, did some samples and so forth, and finally figured out what Rupert was doing to make his carvings.

Kreider's art piqued Bob's creative interest, and he wanted to find out as much as he could about the artist and this distinctive technique, and hoped to see more of his work.

The woman who sold the carving to Bob told him her memories of Kreider's time in Indiana. She recalled that one time when the carver was passing through Bartholomew County, he stopped at her family's farm to ask for a drink of water. Her mother offered him food, and her father let him stay in the barn overnight. Kreider ended up working on the farm for the summer, and for many summers after. The antique dealer lost contact with the wandering woodcarver, and Bob later learned that Kreider passed away in 1983, just two years after Bob had purchased his carving and started figuring out the techniques that produced it. In 2003, Bob saw a significant collection of Kreider's carvings, when the Abby Aldrich Rockefeller Folk Art Museum at Colonial Williamsburg presented an exhibition of eight of the relief carver's scenes. Bob made the pilgrimage to Williamsburg and spent a full day in the museum studying the work of the carving mentor he never met.[4] In addition, he talked with the curator of the show, and she gave Bob all the information they had about the artist.

While studying Kreider's style, Bob started producing commissioned pieces of covered bridges, log cabins, castles, and images of people's homes, all of which helped him refine his own style and skill. Shortly before he retired, Bob began a major carving project that combined a wide range of pictorial-carving techniques. He designed the piece to be a "primer of landscape relief carving." The large scene includes several kinds of trees, different types of buildings, as well as difficult surfaces to render in wood, such as water and glass. He notes that "each one of these features has a different look about it" and requires a different technique "to make it look real (or as real as you can)."

Carved from four poplar boards glued together, the large panel is called *My Town*, conjuring a fictional place where Bob is mayor and all of his grandchildren come to visit him (figure 1.5). A self-acknowledged storyteller, Bob enjoys narrating his imaginative townscape:

> I call it *My Town* and the idea here is that the train is coming to town for the summer. My two granddaughters are on the train and they're coming from Seattle. The preacher's wife went out there and chaperoned them on the train. My two grandchildren from Lexington are here greeting the train. My wife has heard the whistle and is on her way to Bob's Market. She knows she's going to have a few more mouths to feed. My granddaughter Sarah is watering grandma's flowers and watching her sister Leah. And her brother's coming down the street here. He's got a stick in his hand. I think it's hereditary. The preacher's heard the whistle. He's jumped in his buggy here at the church and he's going to pick up his wife. This little gal is from Portland, Oregon, and she is visiting school. It's the last day of school for *My Town*, and she loves school. So she's going to visit the last day. Her brother is here sitting on the fence greeting the train and her other brother, my tenth grandchild, is upside down hanging from this tree here. He loves to climb. So, this is *My Town*. This is 1900 and this is a buggy bridge here. This is a train bridge. It has ventilators to let the smoke out when the train comes through town. (I did say its my town.) I own the bank and the pattern shop and the foundry and I'm the [m]ayor. This is City Hall and this, of course you know, is before cell phones. So I'm not far from the office, I can be reached . . . I'm fishing.

Bob beams as he playfully tells the story of his imaginary village. He points with a wooden dowel as he moves from one narrative element to another—slowly working his way through the entire scene.

Bob completed *My Town* in 2000, ten years after he began. It took him nine years to carve half of the piece, much of which he sculpted in the evenings while working in Wisconsin, away from home. The other half he completed the year after he retired; nonetheless, Bob does not regret taking his time on the enormous piece that measures fifty-two by twenty-seven inches. When he started the carving, which centers on his family, he only had three grandchildren, but when he completed this masterwork, he had ten grandkids. Since he carves from left to right, most of the children are placed on the right half of the board. He

Fig. 1.5 *My Town* by Bob Taylor.

kept adapting his carving and story to accommodate the growing population of *My Town*.

Before retiring, Bob traveled a great deal for his job, making weekly trips to his corporate headquarters in Milwaukee. Through his carving, he was able to keep his family in his thoughts and look forward to the time they would spend together. He stored the unfinished panel in a closet in his Milwaukee workplace, pulling it out in the lonely evenings to carve and think about his growing family. Making the panel helped the carver prepare for and transition into retirement. Through experimenting with and learning Kreider's style, Bob discovered how he could combine his interest in storytelling and carving into a new creative pursuit—memory carving.

Many seniors have made wooden objects in their retirement years in order to remember the past. Well-known Delaware whittler Jehu F. Camper (1897–1989) assembled his carvings into recalled scenes to document past practices and personal memories (Bethke 1996). Aloysius "Ollie" Schuch (1904–1983) of Jasper, Indiana, carved miniatures of the everyday objects he remembered from his boyhood. From small-size wagons and bucksaws, to making a little turnip-kraut cutter and a *schnitzelbank* (shaving horse), the elder produced items once common in the German American community where he lived (Mordoh 1980:22–24; Bronner 1996:129). Indianapolis woodcarver and former National Heritage Fellow Earnest Bennett (1905–1989) also carved wooden chains and miniature farm implements in his retirement years. Directly connected to his childhood, Bennett's carvings helped him share his life experiences and traditional knowledge with younger generations (Hufford, Hunt, and Zeitlin 1987:52; Bronner 1996:59–67). Similarly, soon after retiring, Bob began his first life-story panel: a carved scene that centers

Fig. 1.6 *Mission Festival* by Bob Taylor at St. John's Lutheran Church at White Creek, Indiana.

on one of his favorite childhood memories—attending the Mission Festival at St. John's Lutheran Church in White Creek, Indiana (figure 1.6).

At this church mission festival, he visited with his extended family, and he and his cousins played ball together. He describes the carving:

> Well, when I retired, which was in '99, I had this idea that I would like to carve a memory of the Mission Festival at St. John's Lutheran Church in White Creek in Indiana, which my folks went to school there growing up, a little one-room school. We would go there in the summer to Mission Festivals every year—and so that was part of my childhood memory. When we lived in town, we would go out there. My cousins all lived in and around that area. Most of them were farmers; and so that's a good time.

The completed carving shows the church and school nestled in the woods, and period cars parked around the church. While the adults set up for the festival in the churchyard, the children play baseball. One of Bob's older cousins is up to bat; another is on first base, a tree. Second base is just outside the frame of the picture, and third base is a fence post. More than a static scene of old buildings, the carving presents a lively landscape from his memories of family, fun, and community.

To produce this piece, the carver began by researching the church and school and talking with his cousins about their memories of the place. Bob revisited St. John's to remind himself about the placement of trees and buildings, but the church had cut down the trees in the churchyard; fortunately, he found the stumps and plotted their locations, which helped make his scene more accurate. He then made a 3-D scale model so he could experiment with the scene's composition and perspective. From the model, he prepared sketches for his carving. Yet, like the panel of the Coney Island trip, time had obscured many of his memories of the Mission Festival. He gathered input for his carving from several of his cousins, who had attended the festival when they were young. Through a process of "collaborative reminiscence," Bob and his family recalled the festival and the fond memories that surrounded it (Kirshenblatt-Gimblett 1989:137).[5] There were discrepancies over certain recalled details, though, such as in their recollections of the location of the old pump at the school. Bob had drawn it one place, but his cousins recalled that the pump was in a different location. But when he moved it for his carving, others remembered that they drank from a pump in still another location. It turned out both were correct: there were two pumps near the church and school. Although Bob aims to make his carvings as precise as possible, he recognizes that memories are malleable and fleeting. Through his carvings, he makes his recollections more stable and durable. His scenes though, like many life-story objects, recall memories of a shared experience that resonates not only with the maker's memories of the Mission Festival, but also with others who recall the long-ago gatherings.[6]

Unlike his commissioned carvings and the pieces that he sold to collectors, Bob never intended to sell this carving. Yet he recognized that his panel was more than his personal story—it presented a collective memory valued by others. When St. John's Church at White Creek began planning the celebration of their 160th anniversary, they approached Bob about buying his carving to serve as a centerpiece for their celebration. He did not want to part with the work, but after much consideration, he agreed to sell the carving to the church, and now it hangs in the new glass narthex of St. John's.[7] When Bob created his Mission Festival scene, he had not considered carving other memories. He thought it would be a one-time project, but he soon realized he had other recollections to research and carve.

Though he works in a distinctive style, the pictorial carving of memories is not unique to Bob and Kreider. Perhaps the best-known artist to work in this genre is Elijah Pierce (1892–1984), a barber who lived in Columbus, Ohio, and who told stories and preached sermons through his relief carvings. His works included scenes of African American life in Mississippi as well as religious stories and lessons (Allport 1980; Roberts 1992). Another well-known carver was Cuban American folk artist Mario Sanchez (1908–2005), who created memory tableaux of his Cuban American neighbors in Key West and Ybor City, Florida. The elderly artist focused his scenes on the special moments, people, and places: cigar makers, dance clubs, and front-porch gatherings.[8] Likewise, Bob's memory carvings often reveal specific scenes and stories from his childhood growing up in a midsize Indiana town. However, Bob's carvings differ from Pierce's and Sanchez's work in their detail. Where those artists paint their carved panels, Bob renders each of his scenes in rich, almost photographic, detail.

Several years ago, Bob bought a buckeye log from Hope Hardwoods, a local sawmill, and had it cut to his specification. He uses this wood almost exclusively for his memory carvings, in part because it works easily, but also because the wood's grain and natural staining provides a variation in color and look, which the artist can use to "add interest" to his pictures. This is especially evident in his Coney Island carvings, where the color and grain of the wood give the sky a dramatic appearance. Although he occasionally does subtle staining on his pieces to add hints of color, he prefers to use the wood's natural highlights.

As a youth, Bob always enjoyed trains, and his second memory carving was about his first train ride. He calls the carving *Get on Board*, and it shows people getting on the train. He later revisited this memory in order to carve the Coney Island trip panels, which he brought to the Mill Race Center. He prominently displays the two Coney Island panels in his basement workshop, just above the massive *My Town*. Still, the panels are easily portable, and he can take his carvings to gatherings like the one at the Mill Race Center or to an area woodcarving show.

Woodcarving Shows

For many years, Bob has presented his carvings at the county fair and woodcarving shows because he enjoys exhibiting his work and talking to people about his craft.

> And they always come up and [say] "Wow, how do you do that?" And I said, "I just carved out where the picture is." Then they think I'm a smart aleck, and probably I am. But you know, the Lord gives us talents and one of my talents is to be able to use my hands to create—and I always give Him the credit. I'm just doing what He set me up to do, and that's the way I live my life.

Bob invited me to a woodcarving show in Franklin, Indiana, where each year he exhibits a sampling of his carvings and demonstrates his relief-carving techniques. For the past several years, he has entered his latest memory panel in the show's carving contest. This year he submitted the train panel from his pair of Coney Island boards to be judged. He had completed the carving the month before and was excited to hear the judge's thoughts and comments. Although he no longer sells his work, he still enjoys telling showgoers about his memory carvings and visiting with the other woodcarvers. A testimony to the popularity of his work and talent, Bob won the People's Choice award for his Coney Island carving, as well as Best in Class.

A combined effort of the Indianapolis, Franklin, and Columbus carving clubs, the show is in the gymnasium at the community center near Franklin College. Consisting mostly of senior carvers and their wives, the exhibitors sit behind tables covered with a variety of carved items.[9] While some carve, others shop for new tools and materials. But most of the participants are there to exhibit their

Fig. 1.7 Bob Taylor at the Franklin Woodcarving Show, 2013.

Fig. 1.8 Bob Taylor's carving of a dead whale on a train.

work and visit with old friends (figure 1.7). From wooden chains and chip-carved boxes, to sculptural figures and relief carvings, the artists display their creations. In addition to his new train panel, Bob has brought four other pieces to display: his other Coney Island carving, a small wooden duck, a four-sided relief carving of trees, and an odd pictorial piece of a dead whale on a railroad car (figure 1.8).

As visitors meander through the show, many stop in front of Bob's whale panel; with a puzzled look, they inquire about the unusual carving of a dead whale. Smiling, he shares the story behind this memory carving, a tale he had told me a few weeks earlier:

> One day when I was down [town] delivering papers on Washington Street, a train rolled into town, came up from Louisville, had a dead whale on board. This was in 1941. Actually, it happened to be my birthday on June the third. So, I really remembered that—they unhooked the car, put a tent over it, and charged a nickel or a dime to see the whale.
>
> [They advertised the] largest hog in the world, a flea circus. And they asked a question, "Have you ever seen a mermaid?" But they didn't really say there was going to be one there, that's kind of the way things were. This was after the Depression, before the war, the Second World War, and things were pretty tight. Money was tight and people were doing whatever they needed to do to make a living.
>
> Later on, [I] found out that this was the Pan American Train Show. The whale had washed up in California in September the year before. This is June and they're still hauling it around. A lot of people ask me, "Well, did it smell?" Well, our downtown didn't smell very good at that time anyhow. We had poultry houses, stockyards, the landfill. There was all kinds of things going on in that area, so one more smell wouldn't have made a whole lot of difference, I don't imagine. But, I don't remember it smelling.

After Bob tells his whale story to show attendees, he often answers their questions, explaining his research and carving process.

Exhibiting his carvings and sharing his stories at gatherings, like at the Mill Race Center and the woodcarving show, are important to him because they provide opportunities for dynamic discussions about his life-story art. Just as Bob enjoys the period of reflection and research that precedes his lengthy creative process, he relishes the occasions when he gets to present his carvings and talk about his personal memories and research discoveries. His process of reflection/creation/narration is a dynamic system of reminiscence. Although carving is a solitary act, the elder's work researching his memories and later presenting his carvings are social activities. During his research or discovery phase, he goes through a period of sharing his memories and learning from others about theirs. However, through creation, his personal recollections blend with his research findings to produce a master scene that visually references important narrative aspects. Finally, by narrating his completed panels, his woodcarving and storytelling talents combine into a unified performance.

Walking through the show, I realize that Bob's carvings are not the only memory projects on display. Several of the exhibitors have brought carvings they made when they were boys to show attendees, mostly wooden chains and balls in boxes. Larry Carter, a retired math teacher from Columbus, and Bob's friend, brought a delicate wooden chain with a carved puzzle at one end—a type of carving he had learned from his father (figure 1.9). In his study of Indiana

Fig. 1.9 Larry Carter at the Franklin Woodcarving Show
holding a chain and puzzle ball he carved, 2013.

chain-carvers, Simon Bronner notes that many of the seniors with whom he worked learned to carve "in childhood from a neighbor, uncle, father, or grandfather but picked it up again only after retirement or in old age" (Bronner 1996:20). Where Bob creates remembered scenes, Larry's chain and puzzle materially commemorates his father as an accomplished carver. Nevertheless, both Bob's and Larry's carvings provide their makers with an opportunity to reflect upon and share important information about their lives.

Why Woodcarving?

From ceramics to painting, Bob has worked in many different media over the years; but he chose wood to create his life-story objects, in part because "wood is warm" and has a "soft, homey feel," whereas stone and ceramics seem "cold." Working wood with a blade is instinctual for the elder, who today does nearly everything with a mallet, chisels, and gouges.[10] Each of his carving tools is like an old familiar friend. For example, he has used the same mallet since the 1960s. He notes, "No one would even pay a dollar for my mallet . . . but it sure has knocked off a lot of shavings over the years." Flattened on one side to prevent it from rolling off the bench, the mallet shows signs of heavy use. Some of Bob's sweeps, gouges, and veiners were once used by the "old furniture carvers," who worked in local furniture factories, while others came from as far away as Switzerland and Germany. Holding one up, Bob explains, "This is a veiner that I bought in Switzerland . . . I love this tool." He bought the little v-tool on one of his trips to the Swiss National School of Carving in Brienz, Switzerland, where he has gone to visit with and learn from other master carvers. Whether a local antique or a special souvenir, his tools have a personal connection to the carver. The mallet and chisels have become natural extensions of the carver's hands. His familiarity with his tools, the meaningfulness of his scenes, and the significance of wood as a special medium for the artist all work together to heighten his life-story work.

Many scholars, artists, and clinicians have recognized that making art can be a productive approach for elders to reflect upon their lives, but gerontologists and creative-aging consultants should understand that for some older adults the medium for making their life-review art is profoundly significant. Alan Jabbour, in writing about the role of traditional arts in aging, noted that there is no universal artistic therapy that could be taught or administered to seniors, but that tapping into the power of "folk arts means fundamentally drawing out special forms of expression people already possess, not laying on arts, forms, or programs they lack" (Jabbour 1982:143). In *carving* his memories, Bob employs a personally significant form of artistic communication. Although he sketches his scenes beforehand, those are preliminary creations made only to produce his wooden panels. Carving his memories in wood allows him to extend his reflection on the story and render it through a meaningful medium.

Today, Bob keeps busy researching and making his life-story pieces and other carvings. While one panel is on the bench, another is brewing in his mind. When I last visited with him, he was conducting research for two more memory carvings. The first is a circus scene from when he was nine or ten years old. Like the other carvings he made, he eagerly described his vision for the scene:

> I lived at Eighth and Central—Short Central. The circus grounds was at Tenth and Michigan. The train would come in and be there along Michigan Avenue behind the foundry and stretch back almost to Cummins—that's where the railroad track went through there—which is just two blocks from where I live. So whenever the circus was in town, we'd go over and watch them unload the trains and so forth, and we'd want to water the animals to get a free ticket, you

know, to go to the circus. And they'd always run us off because they didn't want us over there, you know, with all those animals—get hurt or something. There's horses and they've got big hooves. And so anyhow, I've been doing some research on that, and in my head I have that picture now and ready to maybe start making a sketch.

In addition to the stacks of circus-picture books on Bob's drafting table that he uses to prompt his memory and give shape to his design, the carver plans to attend the circus when it comes to town in the spring. He is especially looking forward to re-experiencing the raising of the big top as part of his research. Once he finishes his circus scene, he hopes to carve the Fair Oaks Fairgrounds and Mooney Warther standing on his platform making wooden pliers.

Epilogue

In the summer of 2015, Bob came to Indiana University to demonstrate his craft and share stories at the Mathers Museum of World Cultures. He talked of the red-handled pocketknife, neckerchief slides, and Rupert Kreider. He described his work as a patternmaker and explained how he retooled his skills in retirement to make his memory carvings. He told the stories of the dead whale on a railroad car and his trip to Coney Island. As at the Mill Race Center, where I first met Bob, the students and other museumgoers were impressed when the elder revealed his narrative panels and told their stories. Toward the end of the program, Bob began a new story, one I had not heard before. "This is my latest piece," he said, pausing to pick up a roll of paper from the table behind him. "I was about eight or nine years old, and I lived two blocks from the circus grounds in Columbus, where the circus used to come to town," he started as he unrolled the sketch he made for his new project.

> This is my layout for my new carving of the circus coming to Columbus. The circus tents have already been set up. The calliope truck and several of the cars are still on the train waiting to be unloaded. An elephant is off the car and is having lunch, and the other one is still looking, trying to figure out whether he wants to get off or not.
>
> My friend George is in front here with me; I'm in front here, and this is George [pointing to the two figures in the middle of the drawing]. He always got me in trouble; he was a year older. He is saying, "Why don't you go over there and see if you can get us some free tickets?"

Bob pulls the students into his story as he narrates his uncarved memory. "Well, that is my next endeavor, which is on the table over there," he said, motioning toward a poplar board clamped to the folding table behind him. "Would you like to see me carve?" The group moved in closer.

With his mallet and chisel, he began to rough out the scene. He worked and talked as students and museumgoers asked questions and took photographs with their phones. Before long, the group began to disband, but a few lingered to quietly watch Bob carve. It will be months or more before his carving is finished. After the program, I asked Bob if he would come to a large event at a state park to demonstrate his craft and tell people his stories. He agreed.

A few months later, Bob and I worked together at the Hoosier Outdoor Experience at Fort Harrison State Park. Alongside several other artisans, he demonstrated and talked to the public about his circus carving. That day he was shaping the trees and cutting in individual branches. As people asked, he again shared his memories of the circus trains, hungry elephants, and his friend George, as he had at the museum, but his story had grown. He told of how he researched each of the elements in his carving. He talked of a woman who lived in one of the houses included in the scene, who had seen the carving and remembered the circus. He was proud to have made something that resonated with the memories of others. As Bob and I spent the day together, I realized that his "memory carving" is not just about recreating a long-ago scene, it is a narrative work in progress—a creative practice that allows him to collect new memories. Through his art, Bob has found a way to merge his past recollections with his present life and remain artistically engaged in his community, at an age when many of his peers are challenged by isolation and loneliness.

Notes

1. When Bob first told me about his grandfather and the little red-handled pocketknife, Bob glossed over two points that he clarified after reading a draft of this chapter. First, the carver talked about how his grandfather was a whittler and that he still had the knife that his grandfather gave him. However, Bob had two grandfathers: one who was a whittler and another who gave Bob the pocketknife. The second point was that the carver did not have the original pocketknife, but rather "one like it." Both of these clarifications are examples of how narrators shape and smooth their stories into easily tellable tales.

2. For more about Mooney Warther and his carvings, see John P. Hayes's *Mooney: The Life of the World's Master Carver* (1977).

3. Bob always remembered the fair carver, but it was not until years later, when he and his wife visited a carving museum in Dover, Ohio, that he learned the carver's name.

4. The exhibition was "Life in Perspective: The Woodcarvings of Rupert Kreider." For more about Kreider and the exhibition, please see Mark St. John Erickson's "More Than a Little Whittling: Carvings' Depth Not Measured in Just Inches" in the *Hampton Roads Daily Press*, December 2, 2001. Hampton Roads, VA: http://articles.dailypress.com/2001-12-02/entertainment/0111290423_1_carvings-camps-curio and Joanna Werch Takes's "Arkansas Traveler: Work of an Itinerant Carver" at http://womeninwoodworking.com/ww/Article/Arkansas-Traveler-Work-of-an-Itinerant-Carver-8482.aspx, accessed June 8, 2016.

5. Kirshenblatt-Gimblett observes that while reminiscence can be practiced throughout one's life, there are significant times when individuals may participate in "collaborative

reminiscence" such as at reunions, birthdays, or other gatherings with friends and family, where they can "share their recollections"(1989:137).

6. Varick Chittenden made this point about folk art and shared group experiences in his online exhibition catalog for *Kindred Pursuits: Folk Art in North Country Life*, exhibited at Traditional Arts of Upper New York:

> An artist's ability to recreate memories of shared group experiences is often personal but highly desired and encouraged by his or her group. Great emphasis is placed on precise detail and the object's ability to capture a complete scene or event. Such artwork is often created at a time when the artist feels isolated from other members of the group because of retirement, disability or personal loss (Chittenden n.d.).

7. There is a strong social base behind Bob's woodworking. He is a stalwart volunteer at the Mill Race Center for their woodcarving club. In addition, he carved special pieces for his home church, St. Peter's Lutheran Church in Columbus.

8. For more about Mario Sanchez and his memory carving, see Kristin G. Congdon and Tina Bucuvalas's *Just Above the Water: Florida Folk Art* (2006), and Kathryn H. Proby's *Mario Sanchez: Painter of Key West Memories* (1981).

9. While there were some female carvers and younger carvers at this event, the majority were men over sixty-five. This is in part because of the nature of the craft, but also the group dynamics of the gathering plays a significant role in the demographics of the group.

10. Bob is outspoken about his prejudice against the work of "grinders," his name for those who use rotary tools to carve. Bob dislikes the growing trend of using these power tools. "There are a lot of carvers today, or they call themselves carvers, that *grind*." He justifies his disdain for the use of these grinding tools, in part because rotary tools throw bits of wood and dust all over the user and his bench. Carving with a chisel or gouge is a relatively clean process because it produces shavings and chips in a controlled way.

2 Gustav Potthoff: Death Camps and Memory Paintings

> They call up the past created under present circumstances and designed for the people of the present to view. They are dialogues between the past and the present, and, as texts, they provide ways to investigate such a dialogue. It becomes our work as writers to explore the dialogue between the past and the present in folk painting.
>
> (Yocom 1984:42)

The Memory Painter

Driving slowly down the divided street, straining to read the house numbers, I see a small bungalow surrounded by beautiful flowerbeds; a large American flag mounted to the front of the house waves in the wind. Gus is sitting on the front porch waiting for me. I park on the street and walk up to the elder; his eyes smile. Though I am a few minutes early, I can tell that he has been waiting all morning for me. I juggle my camera and recorder as we shake hands, and he hurries me into the house. Artwork, family photographs, and various mementos crowd the living room. Gus introduces me to his wife, Adele, and then escorts me through the narrow kitchen to his studio, a small room overflowing with more photographs and keepsakes, as well as his art supplies and recently finished paintings. He whispers something toward his muse, a rainbow-colored painting of an angel with a Mona Lisa-like smile. He clears a stool for me, and we talk about his life and the art he makes to chronicle it.[1]

As thick as his wavy hair, the senior's accent clouds our conversation. I listen closely, trying to piece together the stories he earnestly tells me in broken English as he points to his paintings. With the aid of both words and images, I begin to grasp his incredible story of pain, loss, and resilience.

Gus's painted scenes help him tell important life stories, many of which are too horrific to fathom through words alone. For nearly thirty years, Gus's paintings have helped him to maintain a sense of identity, while bearing witness to the atrocities of war and memorializing those who did not survive. By painting his recollections, Gus has developed a blended system of artful communication that transcends the language, age, and cultural barriers he might face in social

Fig. 2.1 Gustav Potthoff at the Atterbury-Bakalar Museum in Columbus, Indiana. Photograph by Greg Whitaker Photography, 2011.

interactions near his Indiana home. In addition, the making and sharing of these visual stories give him a strong sense of purpose and satisfaction with his life—a reason to endure.

Born in the Maluku Islands near Australia, Gustav "Gus" Potthoff was sent to an orphanage after his father died and his mother was unable to take care of him.[2] He stayed at the Dutch colonial orphanage until Germany declared war on the Netherlands; then young Gus enlisted and learned to be a mechanic for the Netherlands Army Tank Battalion in Bandoeng, Java. In 1941, just seventeen years old and only four weeks into his deployment, the Imperial Japanese Army captured Gus, and he remained their prisoner until the end of World War II. While imprisoned, his captors subjected Gus and the other POWs to a brutal regimen of labor that included construction of the Hellfire Pass and the infamous bridge over the River Kwai, both of which were part of the Imperial Japanese Railroad system constructed in the borderlands of Burma and Thailand during the war.

Concerned that the more than sixteen thousand POWs who died would be forgotten, Gus paints to tell his stories of captivity and survival as well as to find peace with his wartime memories by commemorating those who died building the Death Railway. Many may recall the popular movie *The Bridge on the River Kwai* (1957) and its whistling prisoners constructing the infamous bridge, but

Gus's paintings tell a more horrific and more accurate account of the abuse, disease, and death that plagued the forced laborers. Since the end of the war and the release of the surviving prisoners, many scholars have written about the atrocities of these World War II labor camps; but Gus's art recalls the conditions and events in Burma and Thailand as stories of personal experience and reflection, rather than historical evidence and military analysis.[3]

Gus's memory-inspired creations recall and relate his past experiences, which he shares with others. In this sense they are "memory paintings" created as a form of material life review, but also serving as tangible testaments to his past, constructed specifically for sharing his stories in the present. Although recalling and painting scenes from long ago might seem to reflect a preoccupation with the past, in fact these works are often equally future oriented. Memory paintings enable the creative convergence of time. Pictorially narrating important scenes and events from the past but created in an artistic surge in a present moment, these works reflect artists' desire to share their stories and paintings in some future interaction with others. As we will see with Gus's work, a memory painting can be a time-traveling device that carries his thoughts back to the jungles of Burma and Thailand but also gives him a profound purpose to continue into the future.

Although the memory paintings are by definition documentary projects, this is only one aspect of these narrative works. Gus's paintings are multifaceted tools that the artist creates to document past events, share experiences with others, and construct an appropriate narrative about historic happenings; through doing so, he paints to tell stories of and for his comrades who no longer have a voice. In this way, Gus's art is a kind of folk art in that it is deeply social and rooted in community—both the community he forged with his fellow laborers in the prison camps, but also a contemporary community of veterans, museumgoers, and friends for whom he creates and shares his art. Like Gus waiting for me to arrive that day at his home, his art anticipates his social encounters at the local history museum where he volunteers weekly. The creation of his images is a link in a complex chain of remembrance, narration, and commemoration.

"Art Came After I Retired"

"I never know how to paint," recalls Gus. "I never learned art. Art came after I retired from Cummins." The artist taught himself to paint scenes from his mind's eye shortly after he left Cummins, a diesel-engine manufacturer in Columbus, Indiana, where Gus's family moved in 1966. With time on his hands and remembering the promise he made to his fallen friends, Gus's memories of the death camps became more prominent. He felt compelled to tell his stories to a wider audience. He started volunteering at the Atterbury-Bakalar Museum, a small veterans museum adjacent to the municipal airport in Columbus. With his strong accent and gregarious smile, he forged friendships with the other veteran volunteers, even though he had served in a foreign military. Each Tuesday morning he would go to the museum, visit with the other veterans, and talk to museumgoers about his history as a POW.[4] Though he would speak with passion about his personal experiences, language remained a constant issue. Gus had difficulty translating and communicating his memories so that visitors could understand him. Fortunately, he took up painting, which he used to augment his stories and make his memories more explainable and durable. Alongside vintage uniforms, maps, and weaponry, the museum displayed Gus's paintings, which told a more colorful and personal story than could the displays of drab green artifacts of war.

Prominently displayed, the first image Gus painted now hangs in the museum; it depicts the POW camp near the River Kwai, where Gus lived until he was liberated on August 17, 1945 (figure 2.2). Each Tuesday the artist positions himself near this painting in order to tell visitors his tales of captivity, endurance, and forgiveness. The painting shows the final of several makeshift camps that his Japanese captors forced the prisoners to erect along the path of the Thailand-Burma railway. The thatch-roofed barracks stand empty within the compound,

Fig. 2.2 Gustav Potthoff's painting of freedom.

while the bright yellow and red sun shines down. In the foreground, American, British, Dutch, and Australian flags wave above the entrance to the camp, while his captors' flag lies on the ground—signaling that the war is over and the POWs are free. More like an explanatory diagram of the compound than a realistic snapshot of that day, the image does not depict the Korean guards fleeing into the jungle, prisoners peeking out from their shelters, or the soldiers releasing the POWs. Like all memory paintings and other forms of life-story objects, Gus's image of freedom is inherently incomplete, requiring the survivor's narration to animate the scene and bring the story to life (Hufford, Hunt, and Zeitlin 1987:42). Recalling his first taste of freedom in over four years, Gus shared a more complete and personal story of that day than what the image alone tells:

> You know what I do? I like to sneak out.
> And an Englishman come in from Burma with a jeep.
> [Gus starts the story again]
> And I say, "Something's wrong."
> We waited for the Korean to bring us to work.
> We wait the whole day, almost.
> We knew something happened. A bomb, but we not know what kind of bomb.
> The Englishman come in with a jeep from Burma and he say,
> "Boys, stay in! Don't go away—Stay in the camp!"[5]
> But I cannot wait. I sneaked out of camp, and one of the officers say,
> "Gus, where you go?"
> I say, "I go to the market."
> "Oh you better not do . . . What you going to do?"
> "I like to get some good food."
> "And what is that?"
> "Chicken!"
> I needed nutrition.
> Four years in the camp,
> I needed nutrition.

To observe that the above story and painting are narratively incomplete is not to say that neither the image nor the performance is flawed. Rather, the artist plans to complete his paintings through narrative performance and depends on his paintings to assist in his storytelling. Barbara Kirshenblatt-Gimblett observed a similar narrative dependency between her father's storytelling paintings and his verbal narratives. She writes,

> The paintings are not illustrations and the stories are not captions. They are not versions of one another. Rather, different parts of the story are told in different ways in different media to form a whole that is greater than could be achieved in words or images alone. (2007:381–382)

Comparably, the narration that accompanies Gus's art is not due to artistic shortcomings of his paintings, but rather a calculated aspect of the emergent and dialogical nature of his art. His images not only depict the stories that he tells, but beg for narration.

Though Gus was now free, his service as a soldier was not over. The American, English, and Australian POWs went home after World War II, but Gus and his fellow Dutch soldiers were deployed against the Indonesian Revolution (1945–1949). After that conflict, he served nine more years in Holland maintaining tanks for NATO forces. Wearied by years of military service, and wanting more for his young family, Gus quit the army in 1959. A few years later, with the sponsorship of the Disciples of Christ, he moved his family to Columbus, Indiana, where he put his training and experience as a diesel mechanic to use. Though far from the jungles of Burma and the death camps, as the veteran resettled his family in the Midwest, his memories of his captivity remained.

Each evening while his wife worked as a nurse at the nearby hospital, Gus took care of the children. When bedtime rolled around, the former soldier would tell them about the orphanage where he was raised and the POW camps where he was detained. Always careful not to divulge too many details of the cruelty in the labor camps, his narratives of survival became entertaining bedtime stories. Gus told his children about the camps, angels, and elephants. He talked to them about learning to survive by eating what he saw monkeys eat; he described the glowing tiger-eyes in the jungle that watched him. Finally, Gus would conclude their nightly "talks" with a prayer. His daughter, Brigitte, recalls her father telling a funny story about a bamboo-wielding prison guard striking her father on the head; but as she got older, she grasped that behind his comical tales were real experiences of systemic abuse and personal endurance.

Gus's story is one of improbable survival. While imprisoned, he suffered many illnesses: malaria, cholera, beriberi, and snakebite poisoning. Each time, he thought he would die, but each time the voice of an angel would whisper to him, "Not ready for you." He made a promise that if he survived the death camps, he would tell the story of what happened in Thailand and Burma, and of the friends he lost there. Gus honed his stories through years of telling them to his children and grandchildren, and the paintings that explain those narratives are made to help translate the horrific happenings of war into stories appropriate for the families and young listeners who come to the museum.

In the museum, just below Gus's freedom painting hangs another meaningful image that encapsulates his transformation from a young soldier in uniform to a starved captive in rags. Among the first pieces the artist painted, this one chronicles his four-year saga (figure 2.3). Unlike most of his subsequent paintings that tell of specific events or depict a particular viewpoint of the railway, this image gives an overview of his detention and forced labor. Like a mental map,

Fig. 2.3 Gustav Potthoff's painting of his transformation from a soldier to a POW. This image records the camps along the river where he worked.

it records the various labor camps where he lived and worked. He includes the tools prisoners used to cut through dense jungles and stone mountains: picks, shovels, sledgehammers, axes, and saws. The painting shows Asian elephants carrying teak timbers. In addition, the canvas depicts an American bomber releasing its bombs and a Red Cross plane dropping a much needed aid package. In the center, the spirit of the Lord, in the form of a dove, brings flowers to Gus, while his Australian friend sits next to him—sick and tired. In the upper right corner of the image a mushroom cloud rises over a distant land—the bomb that brought about the end of the war; a horrific event that ended Gus's hellish imprisonment.

This image is a self-portrait that permits the artist to cite his past and invoke his precarious position as soldier, prisoner, and survivor. Combining his complex system of visual signs with his verbal narratives of survival, the elder articulates his experiences, confirms his sense of self, and cultivates his legacy as a painter of memories. This work of art mediates the past with the present; it looks to the future and combats the forgetfulness of humanity. However, it is through the combination of his telling personal experience stories with his visual narrative that the painting and the veteran accomplish the goal of remembrance and commemoration. The painting is a compelling work, but its deeper meaning and narrative potential is fulfilled only on Tuesday mornings, when the artist stands forth and bears witness at the small museum. Visitors listen and look as the veteran shares his wartime stories.

A very spiritual man, Gus incorporates spirits, angels, and God into most of his works. White ghostly figures stand on train tracks and trestles, and colorful angels attend to prisoners, while the all-seeing eye of God looks down from above, and the Holy Spirit moves through the work camp. As his daughter, Brigitte, observed, Gus "has a very strong relationship with his Higher Power" (WFYI 2006). The artist painted a portrait of the Rainbow Angel who saved his life many years ago, and she continues to watch over him from her easel as Gus paints. When I visited his painting room, Gus pointed out that she was smiling and that her eyes always followed him. With his permission, I took a picture of the painting; he smiled and said, "She likes that." The painting shows the multicolored angel with a pink, heart-shaped face and glowing yellow head. Through the middle of her body are the tracks of the Death Railway, where Gus worked. Looking more closely, one can see that the angel has wrapped her arms around the starved and ill Gus, enveloping a body reduced to skin and bones. The angel was and still is Gus's protector. Wanting to share his stories and art with school children, Gus cuts out wallet-size, color copies of his angel painting, which he gives to school groups that visit the museum (figure 2.4).

Gus has painted many images of the infamous bridge that crossed the River Kwai, and it has become a common motif in his art. One of Gus's favorite stories

Fig. 2.4 Gustav Potthoff's *Rainbow Angel* painting.

to tell at the museum, though, is recalled in a painting of a different bridge, a small wooden one that he and his fellow laborers built. His narrative centers on a time when Allied bombers destroyed a bridge and endangered the prisoners who were building it. As the planes dropped their bombs, Gus and the other prison workers sought shelter in a wooded area. "We jump and run away behind a tree," he recalls. As they fled, however, a gunner in one of the American planes fired at the prisoners (figure 2.5).

His painting lays out the scene: nearly "naked" prisoners huddle around the trees while the "elephant boy" jumps from the back of his work animal and seeks shelter from machine-gun fire. Gus laughs as he recalls the paradoxical threat from the guns of fellow Allied fighters. Years later, as a docent at the museum, Gus jokes with a veteran pilot who served in the region and who also volunteers

Fig. 2.5 Gustav Potthoff's painting of a plane bombing the wooden bridge.

at the museum: "I outrun your bombs." The two laugh, but both realize the gravity of the conflict. Gus's narrative painting reveals the complexity of both memory and war. Through creating these remembered scenes, Gus strives to recall and understand his imprisonment. Not all of the threats that the prisoners faced came from their Japanese and Korean captors; they also came from the system of war, which can make fellow soldiers and otherwise friendly locals a threat to one's survival, as shared in the next two paintings.

Gus paints ghostly Asian elephants into his landscapes, which is a recurring theme in his work. During construction of the Hellfire Pass, nearby villagers were forced to use elephants to help carry heavy timbers. Gus believes that even more prisoners would have died had it not been for the elephants. The painter's white, ghost-like images of the elephants present them as both work animals and helping spirits. Gus remembers one of the elephant owners, who extorted precious possessions from the POWs. When the prisoners would go to work at 4:00 a.m., the elephant owner, accompanied by his wife, who cooked and made coffee from atop the large creature, would offer tantalizing goods for trade.

"I got sugar. I need your shoes, or I need your coat," the local said as he bargained with the desperate captives. Gus explains that they were "almost naked in that prison, [and] people would trade for nutrition, for sugar—brown sugar and coconut sugar." The men traded to survive, but trading shoes and coats, with no hope of receiving replacements, was a risky gamble that often resulted in sickness, infection, amputation, and death. Once, Gus traded his coat for some sugar but did not lose out on the transaction. When the merchant hung the coat on the back of his elephant, Gus snuck up behind the work animal and retrieved his coat with a long bamboo stick (figure 2.6).

In the painting that recalls this event, Gus includes heavenly light shining down upon him, as well as the host of souls standing on the railway trestle. Gus explains that he asked God to forgive him for stealing. In a landscape of cruelty and treachery, this incident juxtaposes the moral quandary that war imposes on an individual. Gus knew that stealing was wrong, but his life depended on it. He witnessed violence, ill treatment, disease, and death. He saw the inhuman actions of soldiers, prisoners, and civilian workers that directly determined who survived and who died. Nevertheless, Gus paints the story as a

Fig. 2.6 Gustav Potthoff's painting of him stealing his coat from the back of an elephant.

Fig. 2.7 Gustav Potthoff's *Wounded Camp*.

humorous tale of trickery and wit. Just as the elephant owner conned prisoners out of their shoes, Gus cheated the man out of food. Couched in a funny tale, the former POW reveals the hardships of his long imprisonment, the cruelty of his captors and some locals, and the ambiguity of established moral values when survival is at stake.

One of Gus's most agonizing paintings is of Camp 26, which tells the story of the "Wounded Camp" (figure 2.7). The wet conditions and lack of adequate clothing caused many of the POWs to develop serious sores and dangerous infections on their feet and legs. Some washed their wounds in the river, which exposed them to cholera and bacterial infections and made their injuries even worse. When Gus got infected sores, he cleaned them with boiled salt water; while in this camp, however, Gus lost an Australian friend who did not have access to clean bandages or medicine. Gus describes the actions of the camp doctors and the loss of his friend:

He saw your leg off.
Lucky enough, he no do it to me, because I take care for it.

But the Australian, all that he can do is go the river and clean up his wound.
Rotten—You see the bone inside.
And the doctor say, "It's the only way, I can cut your foot, you make it or not,
    [either way] you don't keep your leg."
He has to make a bamboo leg for him.
He had a piece of sock there for the bamboo leg.
He was in the camp there; I was in the camp, too.
Camp 26.

We see all the wounded there.
And I have a wound, but I take care [of it].
I clean it with hot water and soap.

But the Australian, he don't know what to do.
He don't have bandage here,
No medicine here—nothing.

When he lost his Australian friend, Gus buried him in a shallow grave along the Thailand-Burma border. Through his tears, Gus said, "I bury him there, with the angels. He's there. I bury two feet deep, because the Korean don't let me [bury him] deeper." Over seventy years later, Gus still mourns the loss of his friend and fellow captive, whom he knew only as the "Australian."

Survivors have often created life-story objects to bear witness of their confinements and to express their personal narratives of survival. Reflecting on the Jewish genocide, Sheryl Silver Ochayon asks, "Why do many survivors feel the undeniable need to create art?" As she observes, many who endured the Holocaust produced art out of a "deep-seated need." She explains that this artistic impulse:

> may be a need to memorialize those who did not survive—something more
> akin to an obligation. It may be a need to confront the burden they carry with
> them as survivors. But it seems that in any event, for many survivors there
> is an urge they cannot resist. They use their artwork to tell their individual
> stories to the world and to illustrate the atrocities they experienced. (2013)

In similar practice, Gus paints to honor his promise to remember and tell the stories of those who did not make it out of the prisoner work camps in Thailand and Burma. His art testifies to the brutalities they endured.

In 1998, Gus's life and art were featured in an Emmy Award–winning documentary, *Lest We Forget*. For the film, Gus returned to Thailand to see the remnants of his forced labor. While there, he walked the Hellfire Pass, a stretch of the railway that the prisoners cut through a mountain, which cost the lives of countless laborers. Gus saw a huge tree growing in the middle of the pass and was surprised how nature was slowly reclaiming the deep cut through the stone. The tree became a symbol of healing for Gus. After his return home, the majestic tree

Fig. 2.8 Gustav Potthoff's painting of the tree
growing in the Hellfire Pass.

in the pathway became a powerful motif that the artist now incorporates into his paintings. Often the tree stands like an angel in that path of historic destruction (figure 2.8).

On this pilgrimage, Gus visited a memorial to the POWs who died building the Thailand-Burma Railway. Afterward, while walking the length of the railway, he pulled out his harmonica and improvised a tribute to the souls of fallen friends and fellow laborers. Gus was feeling the presence of those souls as he played his song, when a cloud of butterflies emerged from the forest and surrounded him—he took those butterflies to be the souls of those left behind. Once back in Indiana, he painted that memory to manifest the spiritual experience he had during his visit (figure 2.9). Although Gus's paintings are inspired

Fig. 2.9 Painting of Gus playing a harmonica along the railway and the swarm of butterflies that came to him.

by his memories of the past, they are structured to tell important and meaningful stories to others: firsthand accounts of horrific events, humorous tricks, and spiritual experiences.

At home, Gus often sits on his front porch and plays improvised melodies on his harmonica in memoriam. Like his paintings, his music is a creative offering to his fallen brothers and a daily tribute to honor and share their memory. He learned to play after the war, specifically to remember the dead. He elaborates: "I [remember] all the people there and I played harmonica never in my life. Have to do it." So, Gus picked up the harmonica to play his haunting melodies inspired by the sounds of the jungle and the spirits.

Gus built his small painting room off the back of his house several years ago, in order to reduce the fumes that bothered his wife. The room became his studio and sanctuary. Although the presentation and narration of his art are public exchanges, each painting's creation is the result of a private meditative act. In the evenings after Adele has gone to bed and he is alone with his memories and the Rainbow Angel, it is then that Gus paints. A prolific artist, he produces variations of scenes over and over, losing himself in the creative process. Ochayon observed a similar form of compulsive artmaking among survivors of the Holocaust. She enlightens:

> Some survivors use their art to work through the experiences they suffered in the Holocaust—they rework the same themes again and again in order to achieve catharsis. Yet even after they turn to more "carefree" subjects, some sooner or later return to the Holocaust because they are unable to escape its profound influence. (Ochayon 2013)

Likewise, by repeatedly painting his images, Gus strives to recall and reconcile his troubled memories of imprisonment and loss. He constantly paints views of trestles, bridges, and rivers, each an image of a particular scene or place he remembers.

Though he painted his first images with brushes, he soon became frustrated with this slow process. So he cut up kitchen sponges, which he used to paint his memories more quickly, dabbing and wiping the colors straight from the tube. His new method sped up his process and allowed him to recall several scenes each evening. At night when Gus goes into his studio, he says a prayer and starts painting. His Rainbow Angel portrait watches over him, quietly prodding and helping him recall his memories of that distant jungle, the cruelty of the prison camps, and those who were left behind. The artist makes hundreds of images every year, and each is the by-product of his creative contemplations. Unlike his earlier paintings of his liberation or the Wounded Camp, most of the images he paints today are looser and more abstract—the material remains of his late-night recollections. Gus freely gives these paintings away, not just to friends and family, but to everyone he meets. That the recipients remember and share his story is the only charge he asks for his art.

Painting and volunteering at the museum reinforces Gus's sense of meaning and purpose in life. These activities are not mere hobbies that he took up to fill the empty hours of his day (though they do that, too); they are essential tasks that help define and communicate his personal identity as a veteran, survivor, and artist. In fact, Gus often refers to his time spent in painting and telling others about the POW camps as his "work," and he has restructured his postretirement life around these identities.

In his studio hang several personal paintings, including a portrait of his two children, Brigitte and Little Gus, and a landscape of the island of his birth, showing the graves of his mother and father marked by small white crosses. In addition, he displays his night scene of the "taku maru," the small boat that carried him to the camp after his capture. These images reveal that the past is ever present in Gus's daily life. Art is not an imaginative diversion for him; it is a creative vehicle that, like the small boat in his painting, transports his thoughts back in time to his captivity and the death camps of Burma. As in his years of forced labor in the jungles, his memories still compel him to do his work; however, this time he is tasked with remembering, painting, and sharing. He proclaims:

I do my work because I promised to do.
The remembering of friends.
Tell people the story.
And that's what I do for—*just tell people the story.*

Epilogue

In the fall of 2011, I curated an exhibition about Gus and his memory painting. Printed on large nylon panels, the pieces in the exhibit included photographs of Gus and images of his artwork alongside quotes from the artist and interpretive text. First, we displayed the panels at the Ethnic Expo in Gus's hometown of Columbus, and the artist was on hand to talk to the festivalgoers. Positioned near the entrance to the festival, Gus greeted attendees, saw old friends, and told his stories. Gus and I talked off and on throughout the afternoon, but when it came time to close down our booth, and his family came to take Gus home, he did not want to leave. He wanted to continue "his work." Brigitte pleaded with him to leave. Finally, after I told him I was leaving and that I would see him in a week, he relented and went home.

Tell People the Story: The Art of Gustav Potthoff was an exhibition with an opening reception held as part of the 2011 American Folklore Society Meeting at Indiana University. Gus and his family attended the reception along with folklorists and scholars from throughout the United States. Originally planned to be held in a courtyard at the Indiana University Memorial Union, inclement weather forced us inside. Attendees crowded into a meeting room to see the exhibit panels and learn about the artist. After I made a few introductory remarks, I asked Gus, who was sitting next to me, if he would like to say a few words. With the aid of his teakwood cane, he stood and began to talk. He spoke with passion and confidence; although his accent obscured the meaning of his words, the audience strained to understand, and the senior continued to tell his story. After ten minutes, he was getting noticeably weak from standing. I placed my arm around him to steady him as he talked. I offered a seat, but he refused. Finally, his daughter, speaking in Dutch, got her father to sit down, but he continued to tell his story. After twenty minutes of telling his story, he concluded. Some cried as they heard his story, but others became impatient listening to his long and nearly unintelligible narrative. Afterward, however, the audience looked at the panels, read the text, and studied the pictures. I could hear the attendees talk to each other as they saw the stolen coat, the waiting amputees, and the flags of freedom in Gus's paintings, and at last they began to understand what Gus had tried to tell them in words.

Notes

1. I first met Gus when the Columbus Area Arts Council (CAAC) contacted me to see if Traditional Arts Indiana could help "folk artists" in their community. My friend Jeff Kuehl, from the CAAC, and I went to Atterbury-Bakalar Museum, a small military-history center where the artist volunteers. After meeting the artist and seeing his works, I arranged to visit with Gus the following week, which started a several-year relationship where I visited with him both at the museum and in his home. Although this introduction describes my first visit to Gus's home and studio, this chapter is the product of my collaboration with the artist and his family in creating a traveling exhibition titled *Tell People the Story: The Art of Gustav Potthoff*. My lengthy conversations with the artist and his family, as well as in-depth interviews, informed the creation of the exhibit and this chapter. I would like to thank Gus's daughter, Brigitte Potthoff, for being a responsive reader of this chapter, and for providing me with insights into her father's stories and family history.

2. Gus's father was a German POW held by the Dutch during World War I in Indonesia. After the war, he chose to remain in Indonesia with his family.

3. For a concise history about the Thailand-Burma Railway and the labor camps, see Rod Beattie's *The Death Railway: A Brief History of the Thailand-Burma Railway* (2009).

4. Gus makes art for both local schools and area civic groups, as well as to send to museums and veterans homes around the world. While there is a strong social base behind his narrative artwork, the volunteers at Atterbury-Bakalar Museum, like Bob Goedl, are the biggest promoters of his art and his story. Bob and other volunteers helped raise thousands of dollars to produce the documentary *Lest We Forget*, about Gus's imprisonment and art, and continue to sell DVDs to visitors who meet Gus on Tuesday mornings at the museum.

5. Gus has the uncanny ability to find humor and healing in the grim stories he tells. He knew that for the English soldier to order the starving prisoners to stay in the camp after four years of malnourishment and misuse was unreasonable.

3 Marian Sykes: Recalling Memories and Making Rugs

Folk art is a means not only of communication across generations but at the same time assisting the elderly to gain autonomy over their own images.

(Hufford 1984:38)

Introduction

Alone in the front room of her home near Chesterton, Indiana, an elderly woman works at her small rug-hooking frame. Pulling colorful woolen strips through the weave of a piece of linen fabric, the artist fills in an animated scene recalled from a greased-pig contest she attended long ago at a county fair. Having sketched the event onto the fabric base of what will become a hooked rug, she plies her talents to make the scene come alive by hooking and pulling strands of variously colored wool. She has already hooked the outbuildings and farm animals into the rug. Today she focuses her efforts on a small area, the section where the children chase the pig (figure 3.2). Within reach lie balls of colored wool that offer necessary shades and textures for her work. She hooks for a while and then studies her progress. Something is not quite right, so she quickly pulls the loops out and begins again. Work and rework; this is the elder's daily rug-making practice. The hours pass into days, and the days into weeks, until she finishes her memory project and begins to contemplate her next rug.

In making her storytelling rugs, the elder edits her memories and her art to produce rugs that are beautiful to see and pleasant to recall; they are visual distillations of storied events and/or often-remembered locations. Her creative process carries her memories back to "happier times." This is the way Marian Sykes fills her long winter days in rural northern Indiana, making rugs and meditating on her life and family.[1] The independent senior keeps busy doing yard work and home repairs, but in late fall and winter she focuses on her life-story projects when it is too cold to work outdoors.

By conceiving, designing, and hooking rugs, Marian spends months creatively recalling the past and making her art. Through her rug-making practice, she recalls, contemplates, and transforms her memories into pictorial-narrative objects and tools for recalling and sharing her family stories with others.

Fig. 3.1 Marian Sykes holding her rug, *Rima's Bloomers*,
in her home in Chesterton, Indiana.

Through rug hooking, Marian has created scenes of street fairs, family outings, and important life events, each of which relates to a favorite family story,
personal memory, or special place. Her storytelling rugs are a form of material
life-review and the product of creative reminiscence.

An old craft whose roots can be traced back to England, rug hooking was practiced primarily along New England's Eastern Seaboard and in Newfoundland and
Labrador. Today, however, rug hooking has become a popular pastime practiced
throughout North America and beyond. Now, hooking clubs commonly gather at
churches, libraries, and community centers; internet stores sell rug-making supplies worldwide, and patterns and designs are shared through hooking journals
and online communities. [2] Marian did not grow up in a coastal community where

Fig. 3.2 Rug made by Marian Sykes depicting a greased pig contest.

rug making passed from generation to generation, but rather she actively chose the medium to chronicle her life. In fact, she was eighty when she made her first rug after her daughter, also named Marian, attended a rug-hooking seminar and introduced her mother to the popular craft. Having watched her mother crochet and draw for decades, the younger Marian knew the senior would enjoy making rugs. After her daughter gave her the needed materials and tools, Marian taught herself to hook with instructions from a magazine. She made her first rug (a flat image of a sheep) from someone else's pattern, but all of her subsequent rugs are her own designs, and each work recalls a specific life story or a special place. Marian discovered an active rug-hooking club in Chesterton through which she made new friends and found an audience for her stories.[3]

The Rug Hooker

Her fellow hookers (as they refer to themselves) affectionately call Marian their "Grandma Moses," but the artist's pieces are not the rural country scenes frequently associated with the folk-art painter Anna Mary Robertson Moses.

Instead, most of Marian's rugs portray vignettes from her former life in Chicago: inner-city neighborhoods, city skylines, and lakefront beaches.[4] Furthermore, most of her rugs are documentary efforts created to record the years when her children were young, which she often calls the "happy times" in her life. The finished rugs are impressive illustrations of remembered life events, but the importance of Marian's art is as much about the creative process that brought them into existence as it is about the beauty and narrative potential invested in her completed works.

Like Bob Taylor's research for his memory carvings, Marian's rug making requires her to work through her memories and often-told stories. Since every piece is the culmination of months of reminiscing, sketching, and hooking, her creative process merges remembered stories with their visual representations, which produces a unified narrative. Because the maker must choose what to put in and what to leave out, the story shown in her artwork is more limited and fixed than the tales she offers orally. Because these pictorial texts reduce complex storylines and themes to their essential narrative components, the maker augments her rugs through oral narration, providing viewers with additional facts and descriptive digressions contextually shaped by her audience's interest and/or the occasion of the sharing.

I learned of Marian's art when I received an e-mail alert informing me that a new instance of the phrase "Indiana folk art" had been posted to the internet. The Chesterton Art Center was hosting its biannual exhibition of rugs made by members of a local rug-hooking club. I glanced through the post and was about to close it, when I saw the rug that took second place at the show. It was unlike the other rugs on display. Rather than an image of a floral pattern or picturesque landscape like the other rugs in the show, this one seemed organized around a story in that it presented distinct people and a specific place. I was intrigued and called the gallery to find out who the maker was. After several telephone calls and internet searches, I arranged a meeting with Marian and another rug hooker, Barbara Coulter, who helped the octogenarian enter the show in Chesterton and who submitted an article about Marian's art for the *ATHA Newsletter*, a quarterly publication of the Association of Traditional Hooking Artists (Coulter 2008).

A few weeks later, I sat at Marian's kitchen table and visited with the two women. While we drank coffee and ate homemade almond cookies, Marian shared stories about her life, many of which centered on her tragic youth: the loss of her mother when Marian was only three years old, her life in a Catholic orphanage, and the discrimination she suffered as the daughter of Sicilian immigrants in Chicago. The stories she told contrasted greatly with the cheerful and funny scenes she hooked into her rugs. What is the relationship between the troubled tales she tells about her youth and the positive scenes she represents in her rugs? The reason became apparent as we talked about her life and her art. As I will discuss, it had to do with her long creative process of making rugs and the important life-review work undertaken by the independent senior.

Recycling Wool and Memories

Marian recycles wool by cutting old garments that her daughters buy for her at consignment shops and thrift stores into short usable strips. Marian values the quality and price of the repurposed wool compared to commercially available materials at hobby shops and fabric stores. Salvaged material is less expensive and offers a wide range of colors and textures that the artist needs. If a project calls for a specific color not found in her stash, Marian dyes the wool using Kool-Aid or other readily available colorant. Her use of repurposed materials helps differentiate her creations from rugs made by her peers. Not a nostalgic reuse of personal items, like quilters who incorporate significant fabrics from family clothes into their work, but rather a thoughtful preference for old materials because vintage wool is affordable and works well to create her scenes of happier times.

Using recycled materials has limits, though. Most of the rug hookers in the Chesterton group purchase their supplies from vendors, but Marian's rug-making material comes from recycling woolen blankets, winter coats, and skirts, which she washes and cuts into strips. Some of her wool strips are thicker than others, which produces an uneven texture. Although her rug surfaces are beautifully wrought narrative scenes, their backs are often "lumpy." She concedes, "I can never do a clean underside. Instead of loops, it's like little popcorn balls." If Marian's work was to be used on the floor, a lumpy rug might be a problem because it would not lie flat; however, her rugs are not intended to be floor coverings, but rather works of memory art and family heirlooms. Marian does not measure the success of her creations by show prizes or compare her rugs to the decorative ones made by other hookers; she has a different aim and aesthetic mission for her art. The rugs provide hours of comfort to her while she makes them, and operate as narrative devices when she shows them to her friends and family.

In the same way that she repurposes wool in her rugs, Marian reworks her memories into art and constructs meaningful life stories. Just as an old sweater must be unraveled and washed before it can be used in a rug, a story must be taken apart, broken into its basic narrative pieces, purged of nonessential or unpleasant elements, and hooked together into an evocative scene. Marian's projects, therefore, are not just about creating art, they are about reworking and making sense of the past. Current memory research reveals that the practice of retrieving autobiographical memories is a type of problem-solving process through which seniors select, change, and reorganize information to meet the specific needs of their current situations (Staudinger 2001:150). Ursula Staudinger points out that life review and reminiscence are two interrelated social-cognitive activities. Reminiscence denotes a reconstruction of "life events from memory," and life review refers to the process of recalling personal experiences as well as evaluating and interpreting those memories (Staudinger 2001:149–150). Marian's designing and making of a rug might start with reminiscing about the past; however, by creating sketches and through the long process of hooking her scenes, as well as the subsequent narrating of her rugs, the maker has developed a powerful and effective life-review practice.

Rug making and life review are synergetic creative processes for Marian, who only started hooking in 2004 at the age of eighty. Like seniors who create memory paintings, Marian has developed rug hooking into a useful medium for life-story making and a thoughtful process for thinking through her memories. Once she started hooking, she began to recall more stories from her life. Marian remembers, "A lot of thoughts come in my head," which prompted her to start sketching and making drawings of the family stories she remembered. She explains:

> I make sketches until I feel that it'll work. Make many sketches and make a part of it and add a little more. And then, finally, it'll seem to fit and come in place, you know. And I think about what happened at that time.

Eventually, she compiles her narrative components on a transparent sheet that she uses to transfer her pattern onto a linen base with a felt-tipped marker. Once she has traced her pattern to her backing, she stretches a portion of it onto a small wooden frame and starts hooking.

Since each rug takes months to produce, Marian chooses only pleasant memories to recall in her art; nevertheless, the artist has had a difficult life with many painful memories. In fact, she only recently started telling her family details about growing up in the orphanage and the prejudice she and her sisters endured. For more than sixty years, Marian rarely spoke of those years, and then only in generalities.

From the age of three, Marian was raised in the Angel Guardian Orphanage in Chicago, when her father placed her and her three sisters in this Catholic home after her mother passed away and he was unable to take care of them. Marian recalls how she hated institutional life in the orphanage and eagerly looked forward to her Sicilian father's bimonthly visits and the treats and delicious foods he would bring from Chicago's Little Italy, where Italian families lived. Each summer Marian and her sisters were allowed to leave the orphanage and go home with their father for two days, just long enough to get a taste of freedom and experience life beyond the strict rule of the nuns at Angel Guardian. When Marian was fourteen years old, she finally went to live permanently with her father.

Fig. 3.3 Rug made by Marian Sykes depicting Little Italy in Chicago.

Her life at the orphanage and in Little Italy presented her with two starkly different perspectives on life; where the orphanage was controlling and oppressive, her limited time with her father was exciting and unrestrained. She reflects:

> It was like living in two worlds: one institutional and one wild and free. It was enjoyable. But the kids were just out there. There was no air conditioning. There were no supermarkets. No super highways. And you sat on the porch . . . they just played outside. They did whatever they wanted. They ate what they wanted . . . Peddlers came and they brought whatever was in season. So you ate fresh whatever. Fish on Friday and Wednesday during Lent. And it was just a different living. Very, very free. Very loud.

Marian hooked a rug to record her fond recollections of Little Italy, but none of the painful memories of Angel Guardian have been worked into a rug, even though her children have asked her to make rugs about that time in her life (figure 3.3). It would be too painful. She divulged:

> The kids wanted me to do some, but a lot of the things that were at the home are a little painful to think about. I just don't even want to put it on a rug. You know? When you're brainwashed and everything—it's different. I want to be free from that type of living, you know . . . Everything was so controlled and I hate control. I want to just spread out. Maybe one day I will [make a rug about then]; I don't know. I might be two hundred years old by then, but it'd be pretty hard.

The severity she experienced in the orphanage continued to exact its toll on her life, long after she was grown. In fact, some of the hardships she faced throughout her life she traces back to being raised in the orphanage. Years of domination and discrimination shaped her worldview and expectations.

When I asked Marian how making her rugs relates to her memories of growing up in the orphanage, she acknowledged that the process of hooking rugs helped squeeze out some of the bad memories of life in the home. The rugs focus on the enjoyable memories of life when her children were young, rather than the oppressive institution where she was raised. She reasons:

> That's why I put nice [scenes] . . . it's hard for people to realize, they figure you should get over it. But when you're young and you've been hammered all those years, you don't. It doesn't erase from your mind. You get over it in a way—but you don't treat kids like that! You don't make people feel bad.

Marian recalls that life in the orphanage was strict. She remembers that for two hours each day the children could play, but the nuns required the wards to spend the rest of their time working and praying. Furthermore, each day included a scheduled time to punish the children who "were out of line." She fumes, "If you didn't look right, smell right, talk right, you know, they had a beating time. You got beat!" She grew up thinking that strict control was the norm, but once grown, she realized that she did not have to live with pain and oppression.

For most of her life, Marian rarely spoke of Angel Guardian, but after she started hooking rugs and thinking through her life history, she began telling her friends and family stories of life at the orphanage.[5] Her personal narratives often speak of the nuns' authoritarian rule and the prejudice Marian and the other Italian wards experienced. Perhaps hooking the Little Italy rug prompted this change; or the months she now spends in quiet reflection may have cultivated this transformation. Like the rosary of her youth, spending hours hooking and contemplating the good memories may have helped take a little sting out of the bad.

Now Marian spends her quiet days illustrating and hooking scenes of idealized years when her children were young. Though the orphanage robbed her of the childhood she wanted, Marian conjures memories of the years when her own children were at home. It was during these years that the young mother was able to experience the childhood she never had.

> When the kids were growing up was my best time. *I could be one of them* ... And they enjoyed what I was doing, so I did it, you know ... we didn't have a lot, if they had socks that were worn or too small, I'd make a toy out of it. But it seemed like a time when the kids and I enjoyed each other's company. As they got older and teenagers, a little bigger, they were gone. They were different. They felt they knew it all.

Most of Marian's story-rugs cluster not around her own childhood, but rather on the years when all of her children were young and lived at home in an old house on Dickens Street in Chicago.

The decrepit house where Marian raised her family plays a prominent role in many of the rugs that she has made. She and her ex-husband, Charlie, purchased the dilapidated structure out of necessity, when their landlord evicted them from their apartment, and they could not find another place to rent. She recalls:

> We bought it in 1949, that's the year Marian was born—my third child. But there were three buildings in a row. They had one whole face, and it was boarded up. You know, at that time, I couldn't even find a place to rent . . . I had two children, on the North Side of Chicago, and somebody bought the building and we were thrown out. So we bought this vacated building. It was boarded up with plywood windows, and all we had was a big potbelly stove and we stayed on one floor. It was dilapidated. So we fixed it up. I had my third child there.

They purchased the four-story building for $8,500, and Marian worked hard to transform the building into a home for her family. She raised all of her five children in that home and jokes, "Augustana Hospital was right down about a block and a half away. So, I could walk to the hospital, have another kid." In addition, the old house was close to the Lincoln Park Zoo, the beach, and other free activities to entertain her young family.

Marian seldom mentions her ex-husband, Charlie, whom she divorced in the 1960s. Though the couple shared a home, they lived separate lives for many years. Having been raised in the harsh environment of the orphanage, it took Marian a long time to figure out how dysfunctional their relationship was. She seethes:

> We lived on two separate floors. And he would not fix the building. He was not a nice person—very mean.
> And it's strange, you know, the way you're brought up, you realize that people don't live like that. I was raised at the Angel Guardian Orphanage in Chicago. And it was all, you do or die, you know. Very, very restricted and very controlled. And I grew up being controlled.
> And finally, I just had it over my head. But I did get him downstairs by force. And that was the only way we could live until I finally got a divorce, but

it took me a long time, over a year. Every month, I'd take the kids back there [to the court]. He kept stalling, but we put the kids right in the lobby of the court so he could see that the children were there and they were on my side. And they were taking punishment as well as I, and we had it. So, he had to finally . . . So when we got the divorce, he was ordered out immediately and he broke every window in the attic.

Just as Charlie was absent from much of the life she shared with her children and the stories she shares with the rug makers in Chesterton, Marian omits him from all of her visual narratives of her home on Dickens Street.

The Sykes's family home features prominently in Marian's rugs, *Worst Snowstorm* and *Fourth of July*. The background of these two show the house and surrounding structures, while Marian's children play rowdily in the street. In 2006, Marian created the rug that commemorates the twenty-six inches of snow that fell and the week her children spent at home, entertaining themselves by throwing snowballs and playing in the snow. Her story-rug collapses the week of play into one wild, snowy scene, which includes the big igloo her son Richard made, her daughter Barbara selling snowballs to the other children (two for five cents), and the kids building a snowman in front of the house on Dickens Street (figure 3.4). Marian narrated the rug for me on my first visit this way:

> That's the *Worst Snowstorm*. The worst snowstorm in Chicago. I think Bilandic was the mayor at the time and he was in Florida golfing and twenty-six inches of snow fell and wouldn't stop. For one whole week the kids were at home throwing snowballs and everything. They, in fact, the grocery stores on the corner, they ran out of bread and everything, you know, at the time.
>
> But my son made a big igloo with his friend and they had a little dog. They'd put it at the top and it would run out the bottom. It was one of these little mousey dogs. They called him Mousey. And my daughter Barbara was selling two snowballs for five cents so they could throw 'em. But kids were playing snowballs, hitting everybody. And there's the street. And the police were called several times for the igloo on the ground. The kids were noisy.
>
> But that's where we lived. That's where I raised the kids. These were called water flats. So this was the one I owned with the red door. They were narrow buildings, nineteen feet wide, sixty feet long, and you raised your kids there. It was miserable. Very narrow steps, you know—Victorian. So that's my snow story.

Marian explains that she hooked the door to their house in red to "make it stand out a little bit more for the story." The red wool locates the recalled family home, allowing the narrator to easily orient her audience to the storied streetscape. The artist makes her rugs to be both visually and narratively interesting. For example, Marian's rug *Fourth of July* similarly reworks Dickens Street into a fanciful and entertaining narrative scene that blends her memories with her aesthetic sensibility and creative imagination.

Fig. 3.4 Rug made by Marian Sykes depicting the worst snowstorm in Chicago.

Marian hooked *Fourth of July* in 2007, after her son Richard took her to a Chicago hobby shop to buy metallic-colored fiber to make the fireworks in her rug. Also a Dickens Street scene, the storyteller hooked the door to their home in red as before, but in this piece the children have traded in their snowballs and mittens for sparklers and Hula-Hoops (figure 3.5). She describes:

> And that's *Fourth of July*. And that's where I raised my kids . . . with the red door. That was the building we owned. And I raised five kids in that building. That was on Dickens. So Fourth of July, kids would get outside. They had sparklers, Hula-Hoops, kids with wagons, and flags. There's a couple of American flags there—and a bike. I never rode a bike in my life. I never had a bike. The kids did. So, I'm not a very good bike drawer. But I got cats and things like that. And the lady next door, my troublemaker over there, I made her pretty. *She was not pretty*, but I made her pretty. She's keeping an eye on the kids, you know, she's going to call the police on them. But they were all outside.

Making her troublesome neighbor "pretty" was not the only thing the artist transformed through this piece. Comparing the brownstone house beside the

Fig. 3.5 Rug made by Marian Sykes depicting the Fourth of July at family home on Dickens Street in Chicago.

Sykes's water flat in the snow scene with the one in this festive view, examiners can see that the house next door sits back farther from the street—giving it a missile-like appearance. Marian explains, "It was really forward, [but] I wanted it to look like a rocket with the firecrackers." This subtle but whimsical alteration of her storyscape demonstrates the artist's mastery over her craft and narrative. As seniors age, they often have to relinquish control over aspects of their daily lives, but Marian remains strongly independent, and through her craft she reveals her creative ability to make and remake her life through story and art.

Due to her advancing age, Marian moved to rural Chesterton, Indiana, to be near her sons: Charley, who lives just down the road, and Richard, who still lives in nearby Chicago. Nevertheless, she remains very self-reliant. From mowing her lawn to building stone walkways, Marian continues to do much of her own yard and home maintenance. One household project, though, was not of her doing. In the front room of her home, nine of Marian's early rugs hang on display, most of which portray the mother's memories of her family when they were young, including *Worst Snowstorm in Chicago* and *Fourth of July*. Marian may not have intended to display these rugs so prominently in her home. Her other rugs she keeps rolled up and stored away in her bedroom. "Richard put these all on the wall," she says. "It's kind of embarrassing for me to see all this up on the walls."[6] Though the rugs are beautifully displayed, they remind the creator of the elements omitted and included in her narrative scenes. She explains, "I look and I think maybe I should have done something else."

The conspicuously displayed rugs in her living room nag at Marian; they are persistent reminders of the narrative and aesthetic choices she made in producing them. As with all material forms of life stories, some items are foregrounded within the work, while others are omitted or visually downplayed.[7] Although Marian expresses some misgivings about exhibiting these rugs so blatantly, she also seems to secretly enjoy the display, which she can easily share with visitors. Her rug-making accomplishments are a source of satisfaction for the maker, and she takes great pleasure in telling her stories to visitors.

One winter morning, I stopped by to see Marian and talk about her life and rugs. During a lull in our conversation, she looked up at the rug on the wall beside us, an ethnic festival. Wanting to share more with me, she began to inventory some of the meaningful features invested in the rug, pointing out people and emphasizing its narrative elements. "On that one, that's a street scene on Dickens," she began (figure 3.6). "The vendors are selling jewelry and scarves and flowers and things like that. And there's an artist at the bottom on the right and he's painting a woman. He also has a little art piece on the floor he's trying to sell." I interrupted and asked about the dancers in the middle of the rug.

> Yeah, they're ethnic dancers on the street, you know. People watching. And Richard selling popcorn and there's a guy with ice cream we used to call Twinkle-toes, because he'd ring the bell, sell the ice cream, and he'd always kind of dance around with the wagon, you know, up on his toes, selling. So we'd say, "Here comes Twinkle-toes with the ice cream."

Marian beams as she revisits the Dickens Street of her memories, especially when she can share those memories with others. Nonetheless, Marian's rugs are not direct transcriptions of her former life, but rather playful renderings of a remembered place and time.

Alongside her children and neighbors in this narrative frame, Marian includes elements that would not have been a part of that remembered street fair. She incorporates a toy clown and tiger that she created from a cardboard box, as well as a paper-mâché ostrich she made for her children when they were young. Marian also integrated Le Mutt, a small stuffed dog that her daughter Francesca invented. The toy became popular in the 1980s and remains highly collectible, a precursor to Beanie Babies. The toy dog, however, was developed almost twenty years after the time that the street scene pretends to represent. Marian's Dickens

Fig. 3.6 Rug made by Marian Sykes depicting an ethnic festival on Dickens Street.

Street rug does not represent one story, but rather is a mosaic of memories, characters, and happenings that the maker can reference and explain to viewers.

All of Marian's creations conjure locations, events, and/or people from earlier times in her life; still, some of her rugs, like the Dickens Street rug, are less of a story and more about the cast of characters and their distinctive setting for the performance of everyday life. This rug tells of where they lived and who they were, rather than a specific event. The rug presents a remembered scene/context that the maker hooked with a patina of "happiness." The rug facilitates her talking about her resourcefulness of making toys from found objects, the entrepreneurial spirit of her son Richard, and the creative success of her daughter Francesca.

Similarly, Marian made a rug that recalls a time when her children went trick-or-treating, and in it she included popular cartoon characters, ghosts, and an owl, each stressing the imaginative playfulness of the scene. Though she based the rug on an often-told family story, she incorporates these additional elements to accentuate the humor of this Halloween tale (figure 3.7).

And this is *Trick-or-Treat* (Halloween). I thought I'd put all the kids outside trick-or-treating. And right here, the little redhead, that's Little Orphan Annie and Sandy, the dog. I thought I'd throw that in. My son Richard, I dressed him like a girl. So there's pumpkin heads, there's a hole in the tree, and a spook, and the moon, and trick-or-treat bags, and dressed in Indian clothes. But those other kids, cats, black cats, white cats, and a fence . . .

The kids would go to the tavern on the corner where we lived, and they knew they were going to get some money. Maybe nickels, dimes, quarters. And I dressed [Richard] as a girl and I made him padded breasts and some guy grabbed him and squeezed. And he said, "I will never, never, never do this ever again." And he didn't. That was the end. He never even wanted to go trick-or-treating after that, you know. But that was Richard. There's a little owl in the tree and a spook in the tree.

The narrative rug depicts the children outside, not in their Dickens Street neighborhood, but rather on an imaginary country lane, flanked by a wooden fence, tall trees, and scary ghosts. The artist includes no visual reference to the tavern in her story; rather, the rug creates an opportunity for Marian to share the story about Richard being groped in the bar. It is important to note that while the story she tells about the kids trick-or-treating and Richard being dressed as a girl has become an established part of Marian's repertoire, she was not present when this incident happened. In fact, this is not the only rug she made to narrate one of her children's stories. She made one showing the public beach where her kids would go to escape the hot Chicago summers that recounts a story about her daughter Barbara.

Fig. 3.7 Rug made by Marian Sykes depicting her children trick-or-treating.

The rug that hangs across from the Halloween rug tells the story of a conflict between the lifeguards at North Avenue Beach and daughter Barbara (figure 3.8). Marian loves to tell stories about young Barbara, who often gets into trouble in the stories that the elder tells. Marian begins:

> The kids, we used to go to North Avenue Beach, and I got the buildings on the left in the background, the high-rises, and then the fisherman fishing on North Avenue. And then right here is a little tiny gray fish one guy caught. And here's a woman with a baby. My niece, Paula, she was fat—buxom. I got her there and the swimming, the kids, and my daughter Barbara had two best girlfriends; they were twins, Doris and Dagmar. And they were making a lot of noise. They were swearing; they were very bad. And the lifeguards were very, very nice and babysat. And they got tired of them. They told them to shut up. They wouldn't do it, so they stuffed three of them in this wire basket. And threw water at them and told them to behave, you know. And then brought them home to report their badness, you know. So, that was that, but the lifeguards were good.
>
> And there's a little kid running away from mom. She wanted to get a diaper on him. And then the boats and the birds. Kids playing with the balls. And the dog playing with a ball.

Fig. 3.8 Rug made by Marian Sykes of her daughter getting thrown into a trash can by lifeguards.

When Marian told me this story, as with the trick-or-treat tale, I assumed that she was present when these events happened. She speaks as if she witnessed the story unfold. But her son Richard made me aware that at least some of events that she hooks into her rugs were stories told to her by her children rather than events Marian experienced directly.

In many ways, Marian lives vicariously through her children. Appropriating their stories and hooking them into a rug allows her to experience the events she missed while raising her children. With a husband who would not work, and five children to raise, Marian worked as a waitress to support her family. She relished the time she spent with her children. Some of her fondest memories are about when she and her sister-in-law would pack up the kids and drive out of the city and into the country for some fresh air (figure 3.9). Marian fondly recalls:

> My sister-in-law, Louise, had six children and I had five and we would go to White Pines State Park. We were both working as waitresses, had to work at night, so we had very little sleep. But we chose a day during the week where not very many people would be at the park. And it would be almost ninety miles away, I think. Early, early in the morning she'd get up. I'd have to have my kids ready. And we'd all get into this van. No car seat, no belts, so the kids sat on each other's laps and we went. She drove with the kids. They'd start acting up: screaming, yelling, pinching, fighting. And she would drive to the side of the road and say, "I'm going to break every bone in your body if you don't cut it out." So that would quiet them down and they'd shift over, you know, get another kid on their lap. And we'd go to White Pines.
>
> So I thought I'd make White Pines. We'd always get the first shelter in the park because it was easier to get in and out of the park. And Louise would lay on a bench and fall asleep. I would clean out the shelter. I'd get a, like a branch, put some leaves, you know, twigs, tie it up, sweep it out with that. Start a fire. We'd make chicken and we'd have fruit and salad and watermelon. See, I got a watermelon there?
>
> But the kids would run completely wild. I'd make them get me wood for the fire. There was a fireplace in there. See the fireplace?
>
> And there was a brook, so they'd play. They'd go across the bridge to the, this thing, Aleda fell down. You see her little panties there. But the kids, Barbara and Larry, her cousin (my daughter) would be up in that tree. The kids would just go crazy, running, screaming. Nobody bothered them.
>
> So I made silhouette people in the cars and silhouette people in the background. So that was White Pines. And we would, we would stay until nightfall. We'd have graham crackers, chocolate (Hershey) and marshmallow, melted. And that would be the end and we'd go back home and wait for another visit another time. So that was White Pines. But there were eleven kids.

As she narrates the White Pines rug, I begin to realize that like the street festival rug, this piece is less of a story and more of a fond memory. Not a specific visit or happening, but rather a compilation of memories from her family's many trips to

Fig. 3.9 Rug made by Marian Sykes of a family trip to White Pines State Park.

White Pines. The activities in the piece are not humorous or adventurous; they are a mother's reminiscence about happy times she spent with family.

A comparable rug, and the one that hangs next to the White Pines rug, is a piece that Marian made about the free zoo near their home in Chicago (figure 3.10). Not a specific trip or an exciting tale, but rather a general reflection on the many visits she and her children made there.

She recalls that since the family lived close enough to Lincoln Park, they would regularly go to the zoo to see the animals. Her rug includes several lions and other big cats. She describes:

> So there's lions with cubs. There's a panther on one side. And there's a lion doing a headstand, sitting on his butt. There's a tiger at the bottom. If you look real close you can see whiskers, the tongue, the eyes in the picture in the magazine. You can see the face. You see it?
>
> And then there's birds in the sky. And I'm wheeling Richard when he was real little in a stroller. And there's Barbara with the balloon and Marian in the background, and Pie and her brother Charlie didn't want to come. You know, they were too old for that. But we'd go to Lincoln Park, get balloons, a little ice cream and stuff, and enjoy ourselves. And the lady, the vendor in the back, she's selling like hats and things. You know, Lincoln Park. So that's my *Lincoln Park.*

Fig. 3.10 Rug made by Marian Sykes of her family visiting the Lincoln
Park Zoo in Chicago.

Oh, there's a hobo sitting on a bench. And an old lady with her purse,
hanging onto it because the hobo sat next to her—so she grabbed her purse.

Like the White Pines rug, this one is not a story, but rather a remembering or
pulling together of memories of the happy times the maker spent with the family.

As with the earlier pieces presented, this work began as a series of sketches.
Marian kept a book of illustrations that she made about the time when her children were young. She drew the snowstorm, Fourth of July, White Pines, and

Lincoln Park Zoo stories in her book of drawings before she turned them into rugs. A few years ago, she gave the book to her daughter Barbara. Marian recalls the impetus for making the book and how she lost it:

> Barbara, my daughter Barbara, the one I told you about . . . she said to me one day, grown up, she said, "What was I like as a kid?" And I said, "Terrible." You know? Especially a teenager, you want to strangle 'em. But I drew about seventy-two pictures of her from the day she was born till graduation for eighth grade. And then I quit there. But I drew pictures of her getting in trouble, out of trouble, graduating, everything. And she bugged me until I gave her that damned book. And I wish I hadn't, because I could go back in my memory and do more rugs on it.

The senior mourns the loss of her book. In addition to the stories Marian has already transformed into rugs, it included several other scenes that she had hoped to complete. Losing the book in essence resulted in her losing some of her stories and potential rugs.

Despite no longer having her book, Marian continues to make rugs. Today, her pieces often relate to events and places she visited in the years after her children were grown. One such rug is *Greased Pig*, which she made to commemorate the time her grandnephew lost that contest. Her rugs record a visit to an Amish farm in Kalona, Iowa, with her daughter Marian, and even a recent trip to a farm to pick out kittens with her son Richard. Over the past nine years, Marian has made close to twenty rugs, and in each one she invests her artistic ability and hours of serious contemplation about her life, memories, and stories. To view these works as purely aesthetic pieces is to simplify their significance and utility in her life. Through making these rugs, Marian refined her memories and artfully arranged them into meaningful narratives and images. The creative process helps fill her lonely days and provides the artist with tidy stories to tell when she has visitors—like a folklorist who drops in from time to time to check on her.

Epilogue

Two years after receiving the e-mail notice that alerted me to the Chesterton Rug Hooking Show and initiated my work with Marian, I attended the biannual event. During the years between exhibits, I often visited with the artist and talked with her about her memory projects and my research. In the summer of 2012, she suffered a serious back injury while building a stone walkway behind her house. She was in the hospital for several weeks and has never fully recovered. Though she needs a walker, she still lives alone and now works year round at designing and making rugs.

The rug-hooking show featured a variety of floral and folksy-styled rugs made by women from the region. Vines and roses, fall-colored leaves, and sheep in a meadow were just a few of the patterns on display. As always, Marian's rugs

Fig. 3.11 Rug made by Marian Sykes of a Chinese New Year parade in Chicago.

differed from the other exhibited pieces. Though still beautifully designed and executed, her rugs anticipated stories, awaiting their narrator to arrive and enliven them with words. Three of her most recent rugs were on display. Two lay flat on top of exhibit stands raised off the floor. One memorialized her cat, Sophie, who was a phenomenal hunter and had recently died. The other documented a trip to a farm to pick out a new kitten. These two rugs thematically depart from her earlier designs in that they record recent events in her life. But hanging on the wall is her latest creation: a scene of a Chinese New Year celebration in Chinatown in Chicago in the 1960s, which records a time when she took her grandson to the event (figure 3.11). Dragon dancers parade down the street before a crowd while firecrackers explode. In the background Marian hooked the distinctive streetscape of Chicago's Chinatown, which she faithfully copied from family photographs.

I was looking at the other rugs in the show when Marian entered the room, escorting one of her granddaughters to the corner where her rugs were displayed. I was too far away to hear what Marian was saying, but I knew. As she pointed to features in her rug, I saw the same smile and twinkle in her eyes that I had seen when I visited with her a few weeks earlier; she was performing her rug. Several members of Marian's family came to the exhibit opening, including Richard and his three daughters. In addition, Francesca and her husband, who were visiting from Iowa, attended the show. As the family talked, someone said, "I really think her art is improving." Several concurred.

What an odd observation. I had not thought of her art as something to "improve" or master, but rather as the beautiful by-product of her material life-review and a thoughtful instrument for storytelling. Certainly, her techniques and compositions were impressive, but to evaluate her rugs as static works of art seems to ignore the other aspects of her creative practice. Her artistic mastery obscures the true value of Marian's rugs as implements for life review and social interaction. With recycled wool and memories, she has pulled together the strands of her life into meaningful and tellable scenes. She has given material form to her stories and devised a practice that allows her to remember and share stories of happy times.

Notes

1. In spring and summer, Marian busies herself with gardening, yard work, and home repairs. In 2012, she injured her back rebuilding a stone walkway and spent over a year in recovery. This injury prevents her from doing physical labor as before but allows her to design and hook rugs year round.

2. Several histories have been written about older traditions of hooking rugs; for more about rug-hooking histories and methods, see William Winthrop Kent's *The Hooked Rug* (1971) and Joel and Kate Kopp's *American Hooked and Sewn Rugs: Folk Art Underfoot* (1995). Of special interest is Gerald Pocius's article on the social meaning embedded in the hooked rugs of Newfoundland (1979).

3. The rug hookers in Chesterton provide a strong social base for Marian's art. The meetings provide a place for her to show off her talents and share her stories. She especially appreciates the validation the group gives her at the local rug-hooking shows. By e-mail, Barbara Coulter shared her account of Marian's first visit to the Chesterton club:

> I recall our first meeting nine years ago when she unrolled the first rug that she designed and completed. She had been searching for a group that hooked rugs so she could be told "if I am doing this right." It was the farm scene. It was so simple, yet it conveyed so much about life, love, and motherhood. She was working on the Halloween rug at the time and wanted us to critique her work. Her face lit up when we told her there was not a single change that she needed to make. I knew that I was in the presence of a very special and unique artist and I did not want to influence her to change anything.

Marian continued to visit with the hookers, and she and Barbara became close friends.

4. The making of narrative and life-story rugs is not original to Marian; Viola Hanscam, of Harbor, Oregon, started making hooked rugs in the 1940s. Later, as a way to commemorate her fiftieth wedding anniversary, she decided to make a set of rugs for the stairway in her home. For

each step, she made a rug to depict a specific period of her married life. The first illustrated her marriage in 1911. Subsequent rugs show where she and her husband homesteaded and started their family, other places they lived, and stores they owned and operated. The series culminates in a panel that shows the new store their sons now run. Each of the seven steps unveils the progression of time and change. The log buildings and old schoolhouses give way to the modern moment of 1961 when she started her life-review project (Jones 1980:85). Hanscam's rugs differ from those made by Marian in that they were conceptualized and produced as a set, aiming to provide an overview of a life lived. Marian's rugs are vignettes, often specific moments in time and place. Also, the Oregon rug-maker focuses on the remembered landscape through a cartographic perspective, while most of the Chesterton hooker's rugs focus on people within a recalled neighborhood.

5. I have collected several narratives from Marian about her years in the orphanage. These stories, though, often lack the structure and polish exhibited in the stories she tells with her rugs. Perhaps because they have not been refined through months of reflection and frequent telling.

6. Because of the sharp tacks in the furring strips used to mount the rugs smoothly against the wall, Marian is unable to take the rugs down by herself.

7. The act of remembering is shaped by the personal identity of the recaller as well as their cultural values and the specific contexts that shape moments of reflection. Since memory is emergent, when seniors reflect, remember, and relate their recollections, they must translate the erratic and somewhat random recollections into meaningful scenes or narratives. This creative process requires seniors to select, shape, prune, and edit events into memorable and relatable stories. This sculpting of memories is an artistic endeavor, as art critic and historian Roger Cardinal explains:

> Poets, philosophers, and psychologists alike have taught us that spontaneous remembering is sporadic and unsystematic, and that a degree of conscious mental effort is needed to sort the raw data of memory into signifying patterns. So closely does this process resemble the shaping activities of artistic creation that it can be argued that the versions of the past we nourish in our minds, and occasionally communicate to others, exhibit the same characteristics as certain paintings and works of literature, namely: an explicitness of subject-matter, a foregrounding of essential themes, a concern with formal cohesion, and so forth. Further, just as the artistic project involves the rejection of inappropriate or redundant material, so does remembering, in its desire to make sense of the past, rely on its negative twin, forgetting (2001:95).

It is the selection, manipulation, and transformation of memories from daily life into significant life stories that many seniors devote much time toward. Sometimes, recalled activities are monumental, but others are distillations from everyday life that communicate personal histories, values, and beliefs.

4 John Schoolman: Objects, Life Review, and Sociability

Creativity is the common thread through all ages, but worthy of our attention is the motivation that draws old people to material arts. We can increasingly see the use of creativity as adaption. The craftsmen are adapting to changing ways of doing things and viewing things. They are adapting themselves to a new stage of life. As people age, the objects they create change and their reasons for creating change, but the underlying aesthetics they developed in childhood and share with others in adulthood influence how they view the world and how they alter it.

(Bronner 1996:152)

Introduction

At the Senior PrimeLife Enrichment Center (SPEC) in North Webster, Indiana, older adults come together to play games, tell stories, and share meals. The center serves as a daily gathering place for several retirees in the rural lake region of Kosciusko County. A few times each week, a small ninety-nine-year-old man stops in to visit with the others, most of whom are at least twenty years younger than he is. As the small man walks in, members take note of the colorful cane he uses; a woman compliments him on his creation and encourages him to read the poem woodburned into the stick. Afterward, he sits down, and a few more of his friends take turns looking at the patchwork of vibrant colors and words that covers the surface of the cane. Their examination prompts several short conversations between the maker and some of the other attendees. This is a common occurrence at the center: each week, the elder either makes a new cane or chooses one from the large stash of walking sticks he has made over the last twenty-eight years. Each of his works of art communicates an idea, elicits a story, or shares a short poem or proverb; but more importantly, the canes serve as catalysts for social interactions, instruments for interpersonal communication, and markers of their creator's personal identity.

SPEC is located in a large room of an old repurposed school building, which houses several community-based nonprofits. One morning I visited the center to talk with John Schoolman about the sticks he makes and to learn about the social

Fig. 4.1 John Schoolman in his home, North Webster, Indiana, 2008.

contexts of their use. When I arrived, the seniors at the center were broken into clusters. Some sat to drink coffee and talk, while others played cards. The room hummed with conversations. As most of the participants visited, John quietly watched and occasionally chimed in with a fragment of a story, a thoughtful observation, or a funny quip. When he saw me, he promptly walked over to a table where he had placed several of his sticks to show me.

Barb Hetrick, the director of SPEC and an enthusiastic promoter of John's art, sat at the table. She had invited me to the center to meet John and see his walking sticks. That morning, Barb and a few others were studying and talking about two of the canes. One focused on a store John owned; the other listed the names of presidents of the United States.

John watched as the women and I admired, read, and commented on each of the sticks. The maker smiled, said little, but soaked up our reactions. His doting fans asked about the meanings of the various images and texts inscribed upon the sticks; John explained by sharing bits of stories and voicing his personal beliefs and values. While participating in and observing these interactions, I realized that though John enjoys making his colorful canes, their construction is the prelude to a series of narrative events and social encounters that the sticks solicit and facilitate.

In this chapter, I explore the construction and deployment of John School-man's sticks as tools for life review, the impetus for social interactions, and mnemonics for narrating and connecting his past experiences with his present situations. As we will see, John's canes also work to state and maintain his sense of self. These objects are not just artistic products, they are physical extensions of the maker—prosthetic devices that help replace resources lost to age: mobility, hearing, and sociability.

Simon Bronner recognized the interactional and narrative potential of walking sticks when he wrote:

> Canes allow one to proclaim oneself within the constraints of a culturally acceptable form. The surface of this common tool of living can be marked for a distinctive purpose or can frame a particular message. The artistic message, which often presumes narrative translation, might be personal and cryptic, meant to be revealed in conversation with a friend or it could be intended to reinforce social identity directly through the portrayal of shared signs. (Bronner 1992:220)

Though many folklorists have studied the making of canes and walking sticks as continuations of community and family traditions or as creative expressions of personal and cultural identities, few have probed the interactional aspects of canes that Bronner describes.[1] I explore the material behavior behind John's sticks, which, like Gustav Potthoff's paintings, are artful tools for communication that the maker creates to assist with the life-story and identity-making projects of an "old man," as he often calls himself.[2] Some sticks proclaim his values and beliefs, and others assist in sharing important narratives about earlier life experiences.

Although telling life stories is not the only narrative use of the sticks and objects that John makes, it is an important genre of them. The maker uses his works of art as a personal strategy for combating the general disregard and indifference toward seniors that often challenges the sociality and quality of life of the elderly (Myerhoff 1980). Yet utilizing handmade objects to battle neglect and bridge communication divides are not tactics unique to the aged. Refugees might seek to tell the stories of their homeland, testify to atrocities, or articulate cultural identities, as the Hmong do when then they stitch story cloths for both personal and commercial aims (Peterson 1988). Veterans might use art and creative displays to tell of their unspeakable experiences of war, as in the case of Gustav Potthoff. Another example is Michael D. Cousino Sr., who constructs narrative dioramas that recall his experiences from the Vietnam War. He creates these scenes in part to make visible the sacrifices and losses shared by his fellow veterans (Chittenden 1995;1989).

John Schoolman

As a youth, John roamed the fields and forests, chased butterflies, and learned to whistle like the birds. Because his mother died when he was young and his father was busy working, John spent his days exploring the natural wonders near his Miami County home. John grew up with a walking stick in his hand. It was not artfully adorned, but John recalls that in those early years he "always had a stick. Pick it up, you know, to walk with in the woods or wherever—I always had a stick." Walking sticks were essential tools for wandering the woods and fields near his home, as it helped him stay sure-footed and safe.

John lived not far from Peru, Indiana, where many circus troupes wintered when he was young. On his walks he could often hear the roars of lions echoing through the trees, and occasionally he would wander over to the Ben Wallace farm to see the elephants and other exotic animals. He enjoyed the vibrant colors of the painted circus wagons and knew the painter who created and maintained them. Though John's rebirth as an artist began much later in life, his early experiences with walking sticks and circus colors helped shape his later creations.[3]

Throughout his life, John maintained his love of walking in the woods. He continued to pick up walking sticks that he would discard after his daily trek. John shared his passion for hiking and the outdoors with his wife, Ada. In 1936, the couple moved to Bippus, Indiana, to open a store, where they worked together (except for the years John served in World War II, when Ada managed the store by herself) until they closed it in 1973. The couple's personalities complemented each other; where Ada was more vocal and forthright, John was quiet and reserved, or as he divulges, "She was more outspoken than I am. And I just sneak along behind."

For many years, the Schoolmans' store served as a central gathering place and hub of communication within this small farming community. "We had a lot of friends come in and talk," John recalls. "Maybe come over to buy, but they'd stand and talk, maybe for a while . . . had a lot of friends."

It was their advancing years and Ada's poor health that eventually forced the couple to sell the store and retire. By 1976, John and Ada had left Bippus, where they had lived for almost forty years, and moved thirty miles away to Irish Lake near North Webster. There the couple spent their days gardening, fishing, and hiking. When Ada succumbed to diabetes and heart disease in 1981, John had to learn to be alone again, and he began experimenting with decorating the walking sticks he used. He first tried embellishing them with crayons and colored pencils, with little success. Those early sticks he made after his wife's passing did not turn out the way he wanted, or as he would say, "They weren't any good." In the same way, he recalls that the first years after his wife's death "just weren't right," and he had to learn to "settle down" and adapt to his new life alone. John instructs:

> You got to adjust. Periods of your life, you may have to move or something, but you have to adjust to those things. Or some sad thing may happen, you still got to adjust to it, and go on living. *You just got to.* And be just as happy as you can.

Crafting sticks was part of this healing process, helping him fill the void in his life left by his wife's death. Over time, and through trial and error, the sticks helped him discover happiness again: "I don't think that I am ever more happier than when I am sitting there painting one of them . . . I'm just happy." As stick making filled the solitary hours in his life, the attention garnered by his colorful creations also helped combat his loneliness.

The loss of a loved one, the onset of retirement, or another life-changing event often awakens a creative impulse that can lead to a senior making a life-story project. Whittler George Bloom of Dubois County began compulsively carving wooden chains and miniatures of remembered items from his youth after he retired and his wife died (Bronner 1996:36–37). Jane Beck explains that the skills and techniques to produce memory art may have been learned "in childhood, distilled quietly in the busy years of middle life"; but they emerge again when a traumatic event interrupts the life of an older adult (Beck 1988:43). These life-story projects can be coping strategies for dealing with personal tragedy and coming to terms with one's own mortality.

The authors of *The Grand Generation* noted that many of the elderly artists presented in their exhibition started their memory projects in reaction to the life events "that abruptly severed" the artist "from the world as they knew it, or that dramatically heightened their awareness of the passage of time." Through the making of life-story objects, seniors "pull disparate moments and places together" helping to "minimize the fissures created when the people or things on which life depended have suddenly disappeared" (Hufford, Hunt, and Zeitlin 1987:43–44). John's canes emerged as a tactic for addressing this major rupture in his life. His retirement from the general store, coupled with the loss of his wife, triggered a creative surge that helped him through this trying transition.

Although John still enjoys hiking and nature, today he spends more of his time making art. His home is packed with walking canes, staffs, hat racks, plant stands, and wall hangings, all decorated with his signature vivid colors, abstract patterns, and iconic images. Now he paints all of his canes, walking sticks, and other creations with acrylic paints; in addition, he often inscribes them with favorite poems, pithy sayings, or personal reflections that he burns into the wood. Once the painting is completed, he applies several coats of varnish to help protect his designs.

The inspiration for the text John inscribes on his sticks often comes from his experiences and memories of life along the Wabash River, or the life he shared with his wife. A voracious reader and a collector of local history books and works by Indiana authors, he sometimes incorporates poems and quotes from his personal library onto his sticks. However, these quotes often relate directly to his

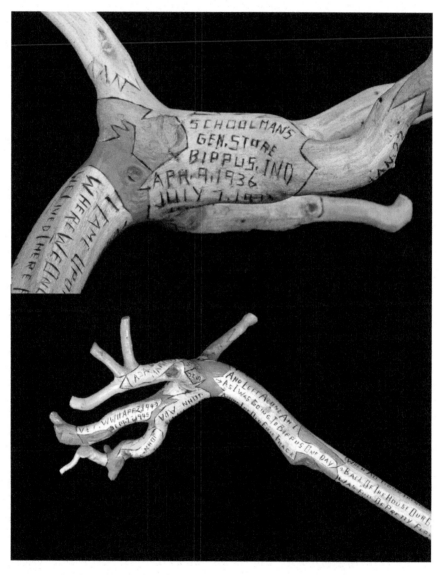

Fig. 4.2 *Schoolman's General Store* cane.

own life story and beliefs. Since the elderly gentleman loves to recite poetry and sing songs, the canes also serve as material crib sheets for his impromptu performances at the center, on the street, or at a variety of other small gathering places. A creative and prolific artist, almost any bit of knowledge, historical fact, or thoughtful poem could catch his attention and become the subject matter of a stick: an epitaph from an old gravestone, the lyrics to Fats Domino's "Blueberry Hill," or excerpts from Walt Whitman's *Leaves of Grass*. Though he usually quotes directly from his sources, sometimes he blends established stanzas and words with original ideas to produce his own hybrids and variants, as he did on the cane called *Schoolman's General Store*.

The Schoolman's General Store Cane

In her research with the elderly, anthropologist Barbara Myerhoff observed "one of the most persistent but elusive ways that people make sense of themselves is to show themselves to themselves" (1986:261). One of the sticks John brought to SPEC to show me is such a work. The cane commemorates the life he and his wife shared at their general store in Bippus (figure 4.2). The gnarled stick combines the natural blond color of the wood with abstract pastel-painted patterns and wood-burned text that fill much of the cane's surface. This is a special stick for John, and one in which he plays several roles in its construction and presentation. He is the maker who caringly crafted the piece, and the poet who transformed ideas and memories into words and verse. He is also the storyteller who animates his creation by reciting and explaining his inscription, while simultaneously being the poem's central character. Each persona deserves closer study.

The general store cane is an autobiographical stick that centers on John and Ada's life together (figure 4.3). Many of his other sticks might signal his values, feelings, and aesthetics, but this one is reflexive and reflective, poetically summarizing the elderly couple's shared life. It is the product of careful contemplation and artful presentation. Understanding the message of this stick is to know something about John and his past life. As with most of his pieces, John inscribed this stick with text and symbols that represent various facets of his life. At the bottom of the cane there is the shape of Indiana with Bippus and the Wabash River geographically marked on it, locating the site of a remembered landscape. Text seared into its surface references aspects of John's recalled life: "St. John's" is the name of the church where he and Ada worshiped, and "IOOF-West Point," cites the fraternal order in which he was an active member, the Independent Order of Odd Fellows. Each of these elements index to a facet of John's former life and creates a potential point of engagement between the artist and the cane's viewers.

The stick's audience is anyone who comes near enough to see the decorated stick that John carries on a daily basis. Whether walking the streets in North

Webster or visiting a diner in Bippus, the elderly artist uses one of his multicolor canes. Like a shiny mirror or colorful feather on a fishing lure, the stick's color and distinctive shape call attention to itself before the motifs and interpretive elements become evident. Once attention is garnered, John is called upon to explain the meaning of the various elements and interact with the interested viewer—it is then that the stick fulfills its narrative function. The visual and textual cues, common talking points for the artist's life story, prompt John when he narrates his creation and life. In addition, the cues provoke questions from viewers, who might then initiate a conversation with the artist.[4]

John wrote the poem that appears on the cane on his eighty-sixth birthday on January 22, 1995. Though John does not often write poetry, he took pride in this composition. He pondered, "I'm not a poet. And I don't know why I happened onto this. This isn't bad for an old man." He then read the stick aloud:

> I was going to Bippus one day along the old Erie track
> I came upon an old house where we once lived years back
> We lived there 40 years, my lovely wife and I
> Now she has gone to her reward and left alone am I
> Back of the house our garden was full of pretty flowers
> Although we were often tired, we spent there many hours
> Our lovely garden is gone now, along with many friends
> Yes, it is the way with life and all good things must end
> Beside the house our old store stands showing many years of wear,
> Where we once sold many things such as ice cream, shoes and other wares
> Pins and needles, steaks and chops, zippers, aspirin, fruit and pop
> We sold it all for many years, and when we closed we shed some tears
> Many years have passed since we closed the doors
> Sometimes I see my friends again when at my breakfast chores
>   —January 22, 1995.

John patterned his verse after the works of two poets, Eben Lesh and Joyce Kilmer. Writing about the store and the products that it carried he borrowed from Lesh, a poet from nearby Huntington, whose poem "Our Grocery Store Man" describes a "grocery store man['s]" romancing of a "hired girl" through the giving of peppermints, peanuts, and chocolates (Lesh 1922). John credited Lesh as a source, but there is no textual connection between the two poems. The primary impetus for the poem, John readily admits, was Joyce Kilmer's "The House with Nobody in It," a melancholy verse about an abandoned home. One has to read only the first couplet of both poems to see the relationship between John and Kilmer's poems:

> Whenever I walk to Suffern along the Erie track
> I go by a poor old farmhouse with its shingles broken and black (Kilmer 1914).

These other works inspired John's poem, but he gives his verse a personal perspective. He recounts the activities he enjoyed with Ada during those store years, offers a selective inventory of the products they sold, and tells the reader (and Ada) about the deteriorating status of the material remains of their life in Bippus.

One interesting phrase in the poem whose meaning is not readily apparent is "Sometimes I see my friends again when at my breakfast chores." The line refers to trips he would take to Bippus to share breakfast with his old friends. He explains with a paced voice:

> I used to go down there to Bippus for breakfast . . . and quite often. And there they were, you know, old friends—*old*. Last time I was down, last year . . . all the old ones . . . one left . . . [pointing to himself]

At his advanced age, John is accustomed to being the "one left." This poem is his only composition that he incorporated into a cane's design, which stresses the importance of its message, sentiment, and theme to the maker. This poem both references his autobiography and reflects the loneliness and solitude that accompanied his advancing years. It was a few days after writing the poem that John decided to make the cane.

John dabbles in many different types of art projects, but cane making has emerged as a defining practice for the senior's personal identity. Locals often referred to him as "the Cane Man." He made many of his early sticks from hardwood, but soon discovered that sumac was easy to work and came in provocative shapes. The artist describes the gathering process this way:

> And then I got onto this sumac; all along the roads, anywhere you can find it. You drive down the road and see [it, and] then you get out and cut it off or dig it out. And I've stuck pretty well to [it], and they're lightweight and easy to work. So I've stuck pretty well to sumac for the last several years. It's easy to find.

Despite his age, when John finds a suitable tree, he gets on his hands and knees and digs the entire root system. Using the figural roots in cane-making is not new to John; in fact, Kentucky folk-art historian Larry Hackley has observed that many of the "most sculptural and inventive" folk-art canes are produced by artists who adapt the root formations into works of art (1988:4). After harvesting the stick, John strips the bark and sets it aside for a few days, weeks, or months until he is ready to decorate it. Usually he gathers his cane-making materials in the spring of the year, because, as he instructs, "if you get it too early or too late it doesn't peel very good. The bark doesn't come off it. After the sap comes up it's easier." For the small sumacs, if he collects them at the right time of year, John can remove the bark in as little as two or three minutes.

Stacks of unembellished sticks lie in his basement, waiting to be moved upstairs where John lives and works. He describes:

> I may set [the sticks] up here and look at them for a day or two or a week or two or whatever. And all at once something will pop into your head and so you start in. It just grows on, and you may get halfway through and change your mind and go some other way.

Once John starts a stick, he concentrates on the creative process until it is finished, working for days at a time planning and making each piece. Throughout the initial designing process, the text, symbols, and patterns on the cane remains relatively fluid, laid out in pencil, until all the words and motifs fit to please the artist's eye.

John creates his sticks at a cluttered table in his living room in front of a large picture window that looks out over Irish Lake. He keeps the table covered with newspapers often blotted with pigments from previous projects. The work light clamped to the edge of the table aids in the lettering and detail of his art. An old cookie tin organizes his paints, while his brushes, a tape measure, and other utensils lie scattered about the table. Like most of the sticks he makes, he began the general store cane's design by writing in the text and penciling the pattern on the stick's surface, which he then painted and woodburned. John chose to accent this stick with yellow, orange, blue, and pink. Atop the acrylic paint, John applies several coats of varnish to ensure the durability of his art and give the sticks a glossy sheen.

On the handle, John painted a goldfinch or a "yellow canary," as John prefers to call it, which heralds the stick's title, *Schoolman's General Store*. The finch and the outline of Indiana have since become common motifs that the elder includes on many of his sticks. Serving as the maker's mark and communicating both his Indiana roots and his love for nature, these icons define the interpretive frame the maker wants his audience to have when they engage with his art.

John never creates his sticks while others are around—he works alone. In fact, one could say he creates *because* he is alone. His creative work is solitary, deliberate, and time consuming. He often spends days or weeks working on a piece. The stick is a vestige of this solo artistic activity, allowing him to bridge the temporal frame between the creative present and the future interactions with the stick's prospective admirers. He works on his sticks in private, anticipating the response to his work in public. He materially negotiates between his isolation and sociability through his creative process. That is, he designs the stick (action) for performance (interaction), expecting that eventually someone will cast his or her gaze toward it and initiate a conversation or exchange.[5] When asked why he creates his canes, John replied, "I enjoy them . . . I enjoy for other people to enjoy them."[6] Simon Bronner studied Indiana woodcarvers who fashioned wooden chains and other objects as a solitary craft and who connected socially by displaying and giving away their creations. "Chains were social tools," Bronner notes. "They were the ties that bind, the carvers' behavioral links to social and personal identity" (1996:131–132). Similarly, John's sticks connect him to the world beyond his memories and his isolated home.

In John's home, finished sticks lie in piles, lean in corners, and fill most of the house. John jokes, "I tell you—you walk into my house and you back out. Basement's full of canes, upstairs full." John has made thousands of walking sticks and other art pieces; but like a book on a shelf, or a dress in a closet, the canes realize their complete aesthetic potential only when they are taken out, used, or displayed. One can appreciate the artistry in each of the senior's sticks, or be amazed by the artful array of objects displayed in his home, but his narrative canes are complete only in use. In writing about similar forms of self-authoring, the authors of *The Grand Generation* note that all life-review projects are "in and of themselves incomplete. They are all frequently brought to life through narrative, the focal points of a vital interchange between artist and witnesses" (Hufford, Hunt, and Zeitlin 1987:42).

The general store cane is the flagship of these sticks, not solely because of its visual aesthetics, but also due to its narrative function. The old cane shows signs of wear from being used often, an indication of its perceived effectiveness, the artist's skill in using it, and the importance of the narrative to the maker's sense of self.

The *Schoolman General Store* cane is a mnemonic device for John's life-review work.[7] From its iconic motifs to its thoughtful text, the cane allows John to share important aspects of his life that are now only memories. The maker has devised a specific technique for laying out each cane that makes the text easier to follow as it spirals around the stick. To facilitate sharing, John marks the beginning of each poetic line or phrase with a small arrow. As he reads the inscription, he slowly rotates the object in his hand. He always reads the entire text of the cane to ensure that his story is complete, sometimes pausing to explain a phrase or thought that the poem prompts. The stick is a mediated form of life review, an entextualized narrative, which the elderly artist can recontextualize in various social settings (Bauman and Briggs 1990:72–78).

By choosing to craft canes, John continues to make and reinvent one of the oldest and most persistent art forms. For millennia, the aged have fashioned sticks to aid in walking, often personalizing them to both identify the stick as belonging to themselves and to make the object invoke a desired personal, cultural, or social identity (Meyer 1992).[8] Though John's sticks are distinct in their shape and style, they are far from unique in their function as being both walking aids and conversation pieces.[9] Many of John's sticks are tools for affirming and communicating his personal history, beliefs, and values. The creation and presentations of his sticks are not mere nostalgic diversions, but rather important statements concerning a life lived.

John's art transcends the routine perceptions of what a cane is, a pedestrian tool, and reconceives it as a portable, communicative event—a device for life review and social interaction. John enjoys being with others and sharing in social activities. He employs these implements not just as a walking aid, but also as a communication aid, which helps allay frustration over his hearing loss and the inability to structure his ideas as quickly and precisely as he once did. He is still sharp and has a good memory, but his impediments threaten his sociality:

> I always like to get out, used to go all over the tri-county area. I've walked all over. (Not anymore.)
>
> I start out real early in the morning sometime. And never hit a big town. All little towns. You find one where they have a restaurant. So, you go in there. All the old folks setting around a big table blathering away. Of course, I can't join it anymore, because I don't know what they're talking, I know they're talking, but I don't know what they're saying. But it's a lot of fun. You do, you do what you want to do. Gets too noisy, you shut it off.

When asked if his canes aid his social interactions and communication with others, John paused and replied, "They help." Afterward, John sat and studied his stick for a long time while others went on with their conversations; soon John had "shut it off." His short answer reinforced how he needs his canes to prompt conversations and help articulate his thoughts when words escape him.

As seniors age, they might need to use a cane to assist with mobility, but John's artful sticks are more than walking devices; they are made to fight another ailment that plagues the aged—invisibility.[10] Unlike the ambulatory aids commonly used by his peers at SPEC, the maker's sticks are specially crafted tools for communication, and as such, are set apart from the common canes used by others. Rarely does anyone but John use the canes he makes for walking, because it is in their maker's hands that the sticks realize their intended narrative functions. It is not that his colleagues at the center do not value John's art; he often gives canes to friends, which they prominently display in their homes. To those who have his sticks, they are objects to be possessed, ready-made heirlooms. For example, John has made over thirty family-tree canes, which he has given to friends and family. These sticks bear the recipient's genealogy but are not made to be used. John remarks, "Didn't get a dime out of 'em, which made me feel good and made them feel good." The sticks John makes, whether gifted or the ones he uses, are social bonds that help him connect with others.

Most of the canes that John produces, however, were created for himself. He fondly comments, "I make every stick for myself . . . I love them all. And I don't sell 'em . . . I suppose I give a hundred or two hundred away." Some of the sticks that John makes, though, such as the general store cane, he would never part with. Occasionally, he would repeat popular themes, such as his Vietnam War cane and the presidents cane, so he could give them away.

John's friends recognize the social and interactional aspects in his canes. Whether at a diner in Bippus, on a street in Fort Wayne, or at SPEC, the colorful canes command attention. Many of his canes were designed to tell stories, but they are also aesthetically attractive, which aids in their solicitation of social interactions. A friend of John's at the center chimed in, "[My reaction] when I first saw John's work is that it's so colorful. I mean it gets your attention right away. And you just want to pick it up and look at it. And then that's when you get to see his message."

The bright colors and curlicue patterns are important visual cues, attracting attention to the stick and telling on-lookers that this cane is different. At first, the seniors at the center do not read the text but are attracted to the sticks' visual appearance. The colors, unusual patterns, and distinctive form of the cane call attention to the object. Once the stick has captured the gaze of its audience, it draws the viewer to the textual and iconic message(s) of the cane. It is then that John is called upon to narrate his stick, read the poem, or briefly explain the meaning behind his words and motifs. At SPEC, these encounters are usually brief.

In some cases, his audience might include one of the small clusters at the center, but usually John's interactions around his cane are one-on-one, and sometimes the performance is quiet and momentary. The morning I was at SPEC,

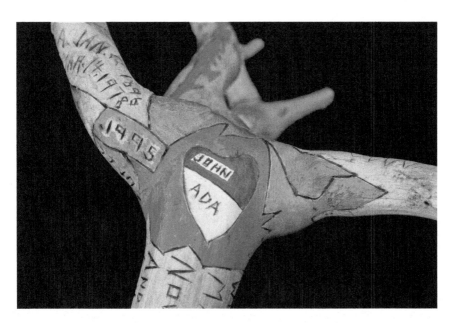

Fig. 4.3 Handle of *Schoolman's General Store* cane.

a woman walking past our table paused and looked at the general store cane. John looked up from the table, his gaze communicated that he was copresent with her, with only the stick and eye contact passing between them. Her only utterance came in a thoughtful, hushed voice: "Pretty."

Through daily use of his sticks, he invites examination, scrutiny, and consideration of the visual, textual, and iconic elements of his canes. Though the feedback is usually positive, occasionally his sticks are controversial, and the response can be "unfavorable," as in the case of his presidents cane.

The Presidents Cane

The canes that John makes often reference his feelings for Ada, enjoyment for nature, and his love for country. The latter of these three themes is produced to encourage remembering. Not to remind the maker, but rather to recall for others past events where individuals made the greatest sacrifice for their country. These "remember" sticks represent the majority of the canes that the elder produces. From *Remember the Alamo* and *Remember Pearl Harbor* to sticks encouraging the remembering of 9/11 and the Iran hostages, John works to memorialize those who lost their lives, especially to recall these events for younger generations. "I love to make those," John proclaims, "'cause they don't teach the kids anything about 'em today . . . I don't know whether one of 'em ever heard of the Alamo . . . and I love to make those things. And I have quite a few of those." Like the production of his life-story canes, the "remember" sticks are constructed not just to recall historical events, but to interpret the past. Nevertheless, one of his sticks is not framed to celebrate a heroic past, but to remind others of the shortcomings of a leader.

In 1998, John Schoolman made a cane to honor the presidency of the United States and to comment on the current president (figure 4.4). The large cane, made from sumac, contains the names and years of service of each president from Washington to Clinton. Still, 1998 was also the year of President Clinton's impeachment hearings. By the handle of the cane are two inscribed prongs that conspicuously protrude. The smaller of the two proclaims the Pledge of Allegiance, and the other indicts Clinton's presidency with text, all in capital letters, spiraling around the shaft:

WILLIAM CLINTON 1993
KENNETH STARR, WHITE WATER
CLINTON LIED UNDER OATH TO THE AMERICAN PEOPLE
MCDOUGAL, BRODERICK
PAID PAULA JONES $850,000
TRAVEL OFFICE, LINDA TRIPP
JENNIFER FLOWERS, WILLEY FBI FILES
WAS IMPEACHED BY THE HOUSE, ACQUITTED BY THE SENATE
I DID NOT HAVE SEX WITH THAT WOMAN. MISS LEWINSKY

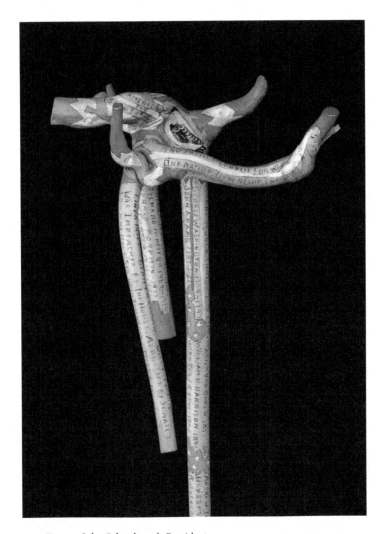

Fig. 4.4 John Schoolman's *Presidents* cane.

This list of direct and implied accusations reflects Schoolman's disapproval of and contempt for the former president. When asked why he made the cane, he said:

The first thing of course was to put all the [presidents] . . .
To put them all on there.
And then it came down to the last one,
And I don't like him.
To me they did something drastic to the presidency
of the United States.

That's just the way I feel about it . . .
I can't help it.

As the cane and his comments reflect, Schoolman believes that President Clinton lied and brought disgrace to the presidency. Therefore, he made a cane to communicate his disappointment and outrage. Still, the patriotic red, white, and blue that attract the gaze of others are also metacommunicative embellishments reminding his audience that the stick is intended to be patriotic—not a blanket dissatisfaction with the American presidency, but the condemnation of a particular president. The short prong quoting the Pledge of Allegiance is a patriotic assertion, yet the phrase "justice for all" stands out as a cotextual commentary to the adjacent branch of the cane (figure 4.5).

As with the general store cane, John is the maker, author, social critic and exhibitor/performer of this stick. Yet the responses that he received from the presidents cane were not always polite compliments of aesthetic approval. Just as the impeachment was divisive, the cane was a partisan expression. Though the stick received positive comments from some, others did not approve. When asked if he used the cane, he recalled:

I used it some and then I put it away . . .
I was in Fort Wayne once . . .
The comments weren't bad . . .

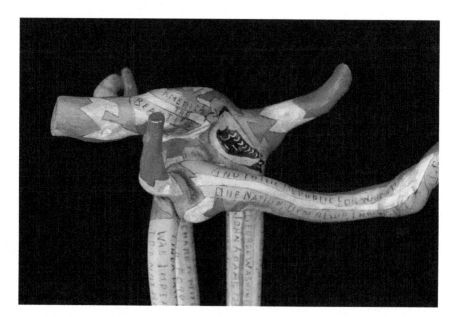

Fig. 4.5 Handle of John Schoolman's *Presidents* cane.

But they weren't favorable.
It's there. [Pointing to the stick]
That's all there is to it.
I haven't had any *really* bad comments.

After John stated the above, he paused thoughtfully. Why did John bring the presidents cane to the center that day? Perhaps it was because that same week Hillary Rodham Clinton was touring the state for her bid in the 2008 presidential primary. In 2007, John made another version of the presidents cane, which he gave to President George W. Bush.[11] The stick prompted conversations about the primary at the center. Director Barb Hetrick joked, "If Hillary wins, she won't be getting a cane." For John, SPEC is a safe place to display and use his sticks, even when they are "controversial." On a bulletin board outside SPEC was a homemade poster with a picture of John holding the colorful stick he gave to President George W. Bush. Next to it was a photocopy of the thank-you letter from the president. Not only was John proud of the recognition, but the center and much of the community also celebrated it.

The following winter, Traditional Arts Indiana hosted an exhibition at the Mathers Museum of World Cultures titled *The Colorful Canes of John Schoolman: Politics, Patriotism, and Paint*. It was produced as part of Indiana University's Arts Week, and IU had selected the theme for the year to be "Politics and Art." My graduate assistant, Selena Morales, and I selected several sticks to be included in the show, and we both wanted the presidents cane to be a part of the small exhibition. On the opening night of the show, I did a public interview with John about his sticks. He recognized that he was not in North Webster anymore, and was concerned about showing the stick. During our public conversation, staged before an audience of more than seventy-five students, faculty members, veterans, and the general public, John and I talked about his art and his community. At one point in the program, John mentioned making his presidents canes.

JOHN: Well, I made one for Bush. I got a note back from him, but whether he wrote it or somebody . . . probably someone else wrote it. They don't have time, you know, to go to individuals—I didn't want to get into politics here.

JON: That's kind of the theme of the exhibit. That's okay. We've got all the different [canes] in here.

JOHN: Yeah, but you haven't got that *one* in here.

JON: We've got the presidents cane.

JOHN: You did?

JON: Yeah. It's out there.

JOHN: Nobody's whipped you yet?

JON: That's why we keep it in a case.

As the audience laughed, I could tell that John was concerned how the presidents stick might be received by this diverse group of museumgoers.

Eliciting quiet smiles and nods of approval or heated discourse and glares, objects and those who make and display them often interact with others through individually, culturally, and socially constructed performances. Whether expressing a life story, political view, or moral belief, John's canes are strong social tools that help an old man to be seen and heard, rather than invisible and ignored. The communicative exchanges between John and his audience are an example of the performances that occur in daily interactions at the Senior PrimeLife Enrichment Center in North Webster. John Schoolman's creation and display events are not large, dynamic productions, but they are carefully and thoughtfully produced. Where the general store cane summons a context in which he can share his life story, the presidents cane amplifies the voice and opinions of a man who has something he wants to say.

One More Stick

When I visited John, he would sometimes give me a stick or some other found object that he had painted and personalized. On the last visit, John gave me a tour through the house, narrating sticks that caught his attention from the thousands of pieces that filled every inch of his home. In the basement, tucked away in a closet, he saw a stick he made to recount a memory of an old abandoned cemetery that he discovered on one of his hikes in the 1930s. The stick quoted the inscription on the stone:

> Remember stranger
> As you pass by
> As you are now
> So once was I
> As I am now
> So shall you be
> Prepare to die
> and follow me
> An epitaph I saw
> On a tombstone
> In a woods south of Mexico, Ind.
> Year 1934—John Schoolman

When these words first arrested the hiker; he pulled out a piece of paper and jotted them down. Years later, after he had retired, he returned several times to the woods to try to find the old cemetery and the stone, but he never could locate them. The burial ground had vanished; either the location was lost to his memory, or nature had reclaimed the small graveyard. John made the stick to remember what he had seen and to share it with others. As he held the stick in his hand, he said, "See like that, when I am gone, nobody will know that."

The sticks that John Schoolman makes are more than the whimsical works of an elderly man; they are important memory and social projects that help him fight the invisibility that many in the oldest generation suffer. The objects also work to materialize the life that he hopes will not be lost or forgotten, like the old tombstone for which he searched.

Epilogue

As the director of Traditional Arts Indiana, I coordinated a few exhibitions of John's art. One was a winter exhibit at the Allen County/Fort Wayne Public Library, where we displayed many of his colorful canes, hand-painted furniture, and Christmas-themed wall hangings. True to form, John brought a stick with an Irish prayer on it because a Celtic duo was playing a winter solstice concert at the library the same day. This show was well received by friends, family, community members, and concertgoers. The second show, the one mentioned earlier at the Mathers Museum, exhibited John's political and patriotic sticks, and included both the general store and the presidents canes.

On the day the exhibit opened, John walked with a special stick for the opening reception. It was titled *A Light Heart Lives Longer.* Since the ceremony also celebrated the elder's one hundredth birthday, the stick was appropriately tattooed with thoughtful sayings about the joys of living a long life. In front of the gathered audience at the museum, the centenarian read aloud the pithy adages, such as "Many good tunes played on an old fiddle," and "I'm over the hill but the climb was terrific." The stick not only played off its maker's age, it also communicated his love for the outdoors and nature. In addition to inscribing the thought "Gardening is landscape painting," he included phrases from the poets he loved so much—Joyce Kilmer's "I think I shall never see a poem as lovely as a tree" and Emerson's "Earth laughs in flowers." In the middle of the cane, though, the maker paraphrases a quote from senior artist Louise Nevelson: "You'll never feel age if you have creative work." This saying expresses the role of John's creative work in his life.

John often noted that he couldn't believe his age, but he was always conscious that his life could end at any time. When we planned the first exhibit, I recommended that we wait until July and do a large exhibition of patriotic sticks for Independence Day. I knew that his red, white, and blue sticks would show best on the Fourth of July. He vetoed the idea; without any explanation he said, "That's no good." John Schoolman passed away on May 21, 2009, at his home. When I heard the news, I instantly thought of the senior's rejection of a July show. He lived his life as if he would live forever, but he also knew his limits.

In the spring of 2009, the exhibition of John's sticks moved from the Mathers Museum to the Center for Folk Traditions, a small venue in Nashville, Indiana, where it remained until the artist's death. After John's passing, I walked through the exhibit while the gallery was closed. The narrative sticks seemed startlingly quiet. For many of them, I had heard their stories, but for others, I could only guess at their deeper meanings and social functions. As I ran my fingers over the *Schoolman General Store* stick displayed in the exhibit, I felt that its story needed to be told. The stick had lost its interlocutor, but its mnemonic properties were still present. I knew it was now time for me to try to tell the story of John Schoolman and his colorful canes.

Notes

1. Sylvia Grider and Barbara Allen wrote about Indiana cane and crook maker Howard Taylor of Dubois County, who learned his craft from his father (Grider and Allen 1974). William Ferris's *Local Color: A Sense of Place in Folk Art* profiled two stick makers: Victor "Hickory Stick Vic" Bobb and Luster Willis (Ferris 1982). In addition, Susan Roach chronicled the effects of public folklore programs and presentations on the art and work of David Allen, an African American cane maker from rural northern Louisiana (Roach 1992).

2. Michael Owen Jones urged scholars to adopt the concept of "material behavior" as a way to look at the creation and deployment of objects from a performance-centered perspective. He was greatly influenced by Robert Georges's 1969 article "Toward an Understanding of Storytelling Events." Jones's article "How Can We Apply Event Analysis to 'Material Behavior,' and Why Should We?" translates Georges's work into a form of credo for material behaviorists (Jones 1997).

3. Focusing on late-life creativity, Alan Jabbour discusses how elderly fiddlers who played in their youth often experience a "flowering" in their playing after retirement (Jabbour 1982). Simon Bronner also observes what he called the "regression-progression behavioral complex," where older adults contending with retirement, age, and perhaps relocation nostalgically turned to a creative behavior from their youth to help them adjust to their new postretirement lives (1996:139). Similarly, though John Schoolman carried a pocketknife and fashioned simple walking sticks throughout his life, it was only in retirement that he devoted time and effort to the elaborate creations for which he became known.

4. For another example of uses of poetic and material cues in memory work, see Joseph Sciorra's writing on Vencenzo Ancona, an elderly Sicilian American poet who created sculptures and scenes by twisting and weaving together multicolored telephone wire (2011 and 1985).

5. In his 1982 presidential address to the American Sociological Association, Erving Goffman encouraged scholars to explore the "face to face domain" that he called the "interactional order" (Goffman 1983:2). My approach is influenced by Michael Owen Jones's notion of "material behavior," which in addition to addressing the "matters of personality, psychological states and processes," also attends to the social interaction related to objects (Jones 1997:202).

6. In his work with Kentucky chair maker Chester Cornett, Michael Owen Jones probed the audience role in aesthetic choices and concluded that " aesthetics concern the perception of and reaction to form, the expression of responses and the effects of likes and dislikes (or taste) on attitudes toward and evaluations of particular forms that are perceived" (Jones 1989:257).

Although John Schoolman's sticks are of his own creation, his interactions with others aesthetically shaped their evolution and designs. He made them for his own enjoyment, but also created them for friends and family to take pleasure in viewing and examining them.

7. Anthropologist William Fenton's *Roll Call of the Iroquois Chiefs* (1950) is an important study of a condolence cane in the collection of the Cranbrook Institute of Science. The work explores the narrative and mnemonic functions of the cane used by Iroquois eulogy singer Andrew Spragg, who used the device at rehearsals and ceremonies of the Condolence Council at the Six Nations Reserve.

8. For another example of reinventing and personalizing old traditions, see Barbara Babcock's writings about Helen Cordero, who revived the ancient pueblo tradition of making clay figurines (Babcock 1986; Babcock and Monthan 1986). The author explains, "Through her ceramic creativity, Helen Cordero has made one of the oldest forms of Native American self-representation her own, reinvented a long-standing but moribund Cochiti tradition of figurative pottery, [and] engendered a revolution in Pueblo ceramics." (Babcock 1986:316).

9. See Petr Bogatyrev's *The Function of Folk Costume in Moravian Slovakia* (1971) for an early example of communication and semiotic functions of material objects. In this study, Bogatyrev noted that villagers recognized folk costumes as having multiple functions; however, one function becomes dominant based upon the context, and the other functions would take a "subordinate position" (1971: 34). Henry Glassie's review essay of Bogatyrev's work explicates the complexities of reading the functions of material objects from a structural or semiotic perspective (Glassie 1973). Schoolman's sticks also have layers of structural meanings. At one moment the stick is a walking device, later it might be a sign of nationalistic pride, or a mnemonic device for telling stories.

10. Writing about elderly Jews in Venice, California, Barbara Myerhoff observed that "the very old" suffer from severe invisibility. The senior community she studied organized a parade and painted a mural to keep from going unnoticed and to share their culture and history with others, who did not know or understand their immigrant lives (Myerhoff 1986:262–264).

11. Giving handmade canes to presidents is a time-honored tradition in the United States. William Burtscher, in his book *Romance Behind the Walking Cane*, recalls how Benjamin Harrison, while on a presidential speaking tour, received a great number of sticks carved by Civil War veterans (Burtscher 1945:122–123). Likewise, James Dow writes that Columbus, Indiana, carver William Baurichter gave sticks to several presidents (Dow 1970:140). The gifting of canes to dignitaries points toward a stick's function as a sign of office (i.e., scepter), commemoration, and political approval.

5   Milan Opacich: Life-Story Displays and Narratives

> Reminiscence is no mere escapist desire to live in the past, as some claim: rather it should be regarded as a major developmental task for the elderly, resulting in the integration that will allow them to age well and die well.
>
> (Myerhoff 1978:222)

Life-Story Displays

The sound of tamburitza music blends with the pulse of the band saw as the white-haired instrument maker works, preparing for his students. Throughout his workshop are several partially assembled guitars, the work of his apprentices. One by one, area millworkers arrive and go to their workstations; the luthier greets them and tells them what they need to do next in their guitar-making project. As his students wait for their turn with the master builder, they often look at the dozens of photographs and instruments that their teacher has displayed on the walls of his workshop. If the teacher notices a student studying one of the pictures or admiring an old instrument, he will tell them the significance of the image or instrument, or more likely launch into a story. The elder's displays are more than shop decorations; they are anchors for narrative interactions. His displays create a place where he can tell his stories.

In clusters of artifacts throughout his workshop and home, eighty-four-year-old Milan Opacich exhibits various meaningful possessions and photographs. These groups of special items serve as prompts for his narrative encounters with the students, friends, and guests who visit his home and workshop in Schererville, Indiana. Through selecting, organizing, and exhibiting these personal objects associated with various aspects of his life, Milan has constructed life-story displays that support his telling of narratives about his Serbo-Croatian heritage and his former life as a fireman in Gary.[1] By viewing the objects assembled by Milan as an aesthetic whole, and by listening to the stories that relate to them, a more complete meaning of his displays becomes apparent.[2] Whether displaying his fireman's memorabilia in his home, or posting dozens of images of tamburitza bands in his workshop, Milan's exhibits have a narrative function. Each object or constellation of objects has its own story or stories.

Fig. 5.1 Milan Opacich in his shop with his first instrument, 2009.

Viewed by themselves, the objects Milan exhibits might seem like prosaic historical materials (i.e., family photographs, newspaper clippings, special artifacts); however, when he tells personal stories and offers contextual data related to these items, he reveals their hidden meanings (Otto and Penderson 1998:82–85). Personal possessions and mementos can be powerful catalysts for reminiscence; even more so, the displaying of these artifacts is often the result of thoughtful life review, and they are arranged and ordered to present specific life stories. Daily, the Serbian senior spends time reminiscing and contemplating his personal and community history through the objects he displays and the photographs he collects. With a steady stream of visitors to his home and workshop, he is often called upon to share stories of his life in the Calumet Region of Indiana.

Recognized in 2004 as a National Heritage Fellow, Milan is an accomplished musician, instrument builder, and storyteller. For more than sixty years he built tambura, a class of fretted string instruments played in popular Serbian and Croatian ensembles. The considered display centers on the first instrument made by Milan and on related materials (other instruments, photographs, and conversations) that augment layers of significance emanating from and invested in this object and its referent story(s).

Milan works in a converted garage adjacent to his home in suburban Schererville, Indiana. The space is part workshop, part school, and part museum, where he builds tambura, teaches luthiery to area millworkers, and collects and displays all things tamburitza.[3] On the back of the door entering his shop, a sign reads "Hall of Fame," and just below are several images: a picture of Milan's brother holding a turtle by its tail; next to it, a photograph of his immigrant mother and father; and nearby, a snapshot of master tambura maker Ivan Hlad. During a visit with Milan, I learned that the people in these photographs are principal characters in a story he often tells about the building of his first instrument. Although these images serve as reminders of the support he received from his family and the inspiration gained from earlier tambura makers, there is more to this cluster of artifacts. Not random photographs from Milan's past, but important interrelated materials associated with an instrument and a story that the artist often invokes to express his personal and cultural identity as a builder within a Serbo-Croatian community. This autobiographical assemblage refers to a story that Milan has told for decades.[4]

In the midst of these historic images is a picture of Milan at the 2004 National Heritage Fellowships award ceremony in Washington, DC, an event that he describes as his "greatest achievement as a builder." Coupled with these older photographs, this more recent one evokes a life story, where support and inspiration from others culminate in the personal success and cultural validation of an artist whose family suffered from community prejudice and discrimination.

Just a few feet from this cluster of images hangs a turtleback *prima*, the first instrument that Milan made. Traditionally the lead instrument of a tamburitza orchestra, the prima is Milan's main instrument.[5] The product of his first attempt at building, however, was "not much on sound," so the maker sold it to a friend several years ago (a transaction he often regretted). That friend gave it to another friend. Eventually, Larry Regan, the proprietor of Jennie's Restaurant in Gary, owned the turtleback prima, which he displayed at his restaurant as a decoration and cultural marker (March 1977:129). In the 1970s, Milan explained to folklorist Richard Dorson why he had sold it:

> It turned out so bad that I gave it to Jack. Jack gave it to a friend who gave it to another friend. And it winds up now it belongs to Larry Regan, that we're playing in his little restaurant on 34th and Broadway. I liked to have it back so I could bury it in the backyard. (Dorson 1981:160–161)

Years later, Regan walked into Milan's shop and wanted to trade the original prima for a handmade guitar, to which the maker happily agreed. However, Milan did *not* "bury it in the backyard." Instead, he prominently displayed the turtleback prima on his shop wall, next to the second instrument that he made and the photographs.

The instrument and these images resonate in chorus, naturally summoning a story from the senior (figure 5.2). When I first noticed the photograph of

Milan's brother, having heard the story of the prima before, Milan and I had this brief exchange:

> JON: Is that a picture of your brother with the turtle?
> MILAN: Yeah, that is my late brother,
> with the very first instrument that I made.
> Local species of a turtle that we ate.
> And I made my first instrument.
> And it hangs on the wall over there.
> It's really a dud, but at least it got me started.

As Milan summarized, he spoke in a staccato voice as if checking off a list of abstract points in a story that he has told many times. I immediately realized that the entryway to his shop was a carefully constructed site for telling this story. The threads of Milan's outlined narrative, the object it narrates, and the assemblage of related objects are important expressions of his personal and cultural identity.

This chapter unites the study of personal experience narratives with the life-story exhibits of older adults. The creation of home displays by elders is a common and underappreciated aesthetic practice. Through Milan, I explore the use and meaning of a display made by an instrument maker who assembled and arranged personal artifacts that reference an often-told story. By exhibiting his

Fig. 5.2 Display on the back of the door to Milan's shop in Schererville, Indiana, 2007.

meaningful possessions in relational clusters, the senior has optimized a story-telling space, where he is called upon to share his narrative.

Material objects have the capacity to communicate a maker's cultural identity, an owner's social status, or a collector's peculiar interests. Nevertheless, as ethnologist Bjarne Rogan has observed, the "role of objects as keepers of their owners personal life histories is underestimated in discussions on material culture," especially in the lives of older adults (Rogan 1998:94). Although some facets of an object's meaning are culturally bound and widely known, other aspects require individual explication and narration to be understood. In fact, often elders strategically place their personal collections and special objects in public view to create opportunities for sharing personal beliefs and life stories. Lene Otto and Lykke Penderson note that personal collections of artifacts constitute a type of life history. They explain:

> Every collection, however small and insignificant it might be, constitutes a personal narrative by virtue of its selection, composition and ordering principles. From the individual things that are associated with different parts of the life course, a coherent narrative is constructed. The objects create memory, and the narrative links time and life. Without the specifics and personal background history, however, the cultural-historical value of the memories disappears and they become banal survivals. (Otto and Penderson 1998:84–85)

The story and meanings associated with these collections are not always evident, and they beg for their curator to narrate their stories and explain their importance.

The son of a Croatian mother (Roza Opacich) and a Serbian father (Mile Opacich), Milan was born in Gary, Indiana, in 1928. Religious and political conflicts between Serbians and Croatians were persistent when he was growing up in the Calumet Region, which is home to one of the largest Serbo-Croatian communities in the United States.[6] Being a "half-breed," as he jokingly refers to himself, positioned Milan on the cultural boundary between both communities, where his family bore the brunt of ethnic and religious prejudice. His mother was not allowed to worship with the Croatian Catholics because she had married a Serbian. His father chose not to worship at the Serbian Orthodox Church because they did not accept Milan's mother. Religious and ethnic differences divided his community, so Milan used music, art, and stories to bring together his family and friends and combat the discrimination he faced.

Living within this large enclave of South Slavic immigrants, Milan heard the music of tamburitza orchestras playing at neighborhood gatherings. Tambura and *gusles* leaned in corners of living rooms or hung on walls as symbols of national and ethnic identity. At around four years of age, he remembers playing with an old prima at the home of a Gary couple until its owner scolded him. The tambura was musically, materially, and symbolically a persistent part of his early life.

Though he grew up during the Depression, Milan's parents encouraged his interest in music. He recalls:

Well, I always like to give my dad the credit for my building.
Because as a youngster they bought me three or four ukuleles,
which I managed to demolish in a matter of hours.
It was hard times. It was the Depression.

So after three ukes, they couldn't afford to buy me any more.
So my dad, (who was quite a craftsman in his own right),
fashioned me a prima out of plywood and strung it up with rubber bands.
And I watched this whole procedure.
And I think somewhere in the back of my mind,
he created this desire for me to be able to do this.[7]

In addition to the tamburitza music Milan heard at community gatherings, country music flowed into his home from Chicago radio stations. By eighteen, he had taught himself to play guitar and formed a country band called the Opossum Holler Ramblers, which featured four youths playing guitars, electric mandolin,

Fig. 5.3 Milan Opacich and the Drina Orchestra playing at the Jovial Club in East Chicago, Indiana, 2005.

and washtub bass. Despite his interest in country music, Milan started a tamburitza band called the Continentals, which employed a mix of experienced Serbian, Croatian, and Irish musicians. The eclectic band "played music of all nationalities, pop tunes, even a few country songs." Milan liked playing tamburitza; while club owners usually paid the country band in beer, the tamburitza musicians were tipped well by listeners who wanted to hear music that reflected their ethnic and national identities. For more than sixty years, Milan played tamburitza music, much of it with his ethnically diverse Drina Orchestra, which provided music for social clubs, weddings, and festivals throughout the Chicagoland area (figure 5.3). When Milan retired from the orchestra in 2006, the band was still ethnically blended: three of his bandmates had Serbian fathers, and three had Croatian fathers. Milan commented about the diversity of his group: "Only in America could this happen." By choosing a varied repertoire of songs and assembling an ethnically mixed band, Milan worked for decades to desegregate his community while still embracing his Serbo-Croatian identity through tamburitza.

"Well, the first prima player that I played with," Milan remembers, "played on a turtleback instrument, and I was enthralled by a turtleback prima." Inspired by his friend's prima, the young musician purchased one with a wood body from the Velentich Brothers in Pittsburgh.[8] Before long, however, the instrument "went sour," and in 1949, he visited the workshop of Ivan Hlad, a well-known Chicago tambura maker, to get it fixed. Milan recalls:

> I wanted to get it fixed. So I took it to Hlad in Chicago and he examined it.
> And these were his exact words:
> "Who make-a this base-a-ball bat?"
> So he goes to the window and pulls out this turtle shell that he just finished for
>   some guy that was supposed to get it, but was drafted in the army and now
>   it was up for grabs, and I got it.
> Jon: Right. So, you got it. Was that before you made your own prima?
> Milan: Yes, that came later.
> You know, visiting his shop, he put a little bug in me
> and I got very interested in this.
> He was not the type to build a little fire in you to want to do anything like this.

A master builder, Hlad had apprenticed in Graz, Austria, and like many other older tambura makers, he was secretive about his craft. Milan's parents loaned their son the money to purchase the Hlad prima, which "played like a Stradivari" compared to the Velentich prima. Milan performed with the Hlad instrument for many years. His daughter Karin used it in a junior tamburitza group, and today it hangs in Milan's music room with several other collectible instruments.

With a strong background in music and inspired by his father and Hlad, Milan wanted to make a prima for himself. As an adult, he apprenticed as a tool-and-die maker at Gary Screw and Bolt Works, where he learned a machin-ist's trade. Milan might have had the inspiration, desire, and tools to make a turtleback prima, but he still needed the turtle! Therefore, he enlisted the aid of his brother. An avid storyteller, Milan often explicates his ideas through the narratives he tells, and one of his favorite stories is about how he and his brother procured the turtle for his first prima from a Valparaiso Swamp.[9] More than once while standing in Milan's shop looking at the photographs or studying the unusual-looking instrument on the wall, I heard him tell this story to a student, visitor, or as in the case below, a folklorist with a recorder.

> My brother had a friend in Valparaiso that had a farm,
> and on that farm they had this swamp.
> And the owner said there were turtles galore in this swamp.
> So, we ventured to Valparaiso.
> My brother, who was an expert marksman with a gun; we sat on the shore; and
>   one raised its head, and he nailed it.
>
> And he jumps into this god-awful looking swamp going after the prima, and he
>   encourages me to follow him.
> I'm not a swimmer and I don't like swamp water.
> But I go, I go in with him,
> By tapping with his foot, he locates this turtle.
> Picks it up by the tail and walks out of the swamp, and I have my . . .
> I have my turtle now.
> The only problem is now,
> he shot it right through the head,
> —but it's still walking around!
>
> My brother was the type of guy,
> He was a hunter.
> What you hunted, you ate.
> So if he shot a lot of rabbits,
> I had to clean the rabbits, and we had rabbits.
> He did squirrels, I did that.
> Now I've got this turtle, I'm going to be the turtle cleaner now.
> Little more complicated than that.
> So we enlisted the aid of a neighbor who had experience with turtles,
> and he got the meat of the turtle out.
>
> And my mom, (to keep peace in the family),
> she made a wonderful soup out of it.
> I didn't care so much for the meat, but the soup was good.
> But I think what probably threw me off kilter was,
> I looked into the pot after about three hours of boiling on the stove [shakes head],

I lifted the lid, and there's this,
—the turtle legs are still churning in this soup!
I told my brother,
I said, "I don't think I am going to like this meal."
But I managed to get the soup down.

And from this turtle shell, I took it to the plant where I worked.
And made that instrument on government time, which is your lunch hour.

I was able to make the scroll head.
And I did it with files.
I still don't know how I did that.
After I completed the instrument, it was not much on sound,
but it was an incentive to go ahead and make a number two instrument,
which I made out of wood, and I did get better results with that one.
And it seemed like each instrument I made, I seemed to progress a little bit
    better.
To the point where now I think I've probably reached my peak.
If there's any better primas made, someone else is going to have to make them.

This telling of the story occurred during a videotaped interview that I conducted with Milan in 2005. Videographer Anders Lund and I had been at the artist's home for two days documenting the making of a small "G" prima.[10] Nevertheless, Milan has told the turtle story many times and for many occasions. Richard March collected a version of Milan's turtle tale while working on the Gary Project, a student-powered fieldwork initiative from Indiana University's Folklore Institute in the 1970s (137–138). Richard Dorson included a version of the account in his classic text, *Land of the Millrats* (1981:159–164). Milan also shared the turtle story with visitors on the National Mall at the Festival of American Folklife in 1976, and then again in 1981. He told it to me the first time I visited his shop in 2004, and has shared it with countless other folklorists, reporters, historians, neighbors, musicians, and would-be luthiers.

The images and instrument on display invite inquiry that has often led to the telling of this tale. For many years, Milan has taught guitar-making for JobLink, a vocational training program that supports the life-long learning of steel-mill workers in the region. As students from the mills visit the shop, the white-haired luthier teaches them not just to build and repair instruments, but with the aid of his artifactual display, he tells them the story of the Slavic heritage of the region and his personal narrative of achievement. The doorway provides more than just an entrance to his shop; it gives visitors an entrée into the elder's life history and creates a stage where he can share his special story of family support and perseverance.

Milan often answers the millworkers' questions with a short story, drawing upon his life history to impart wisdom and make points. Patrick Mullen observed that when older adults review and interpret their lives through stories, a "pattern of symbolic meaning," or what he calls "themes," emerges.

> When the narratives that make up a life story and meaningful objects and rituals in a person's life (personal photographs, memorabilia, quilts, foodways, folk medical practices, etc.) are viewed together certain recurring themes become apparent. These themes unify the various strands of the story, relating the images, metaphors, and symbols together around the central meaning. (1992:14–15)

The above telling of the turtle narrative reveals three persistent themes that I realized are present in many of his narratives and supported by his life-story display: the importance of familial support, the transformative power of knowledge and skill, and a belief that future success grows from inspiration.

Milan's narrative themes are not just motifs or storytelling devices; they reflect his personal and creative values, which influence not just his storytelling, but also the type of music he plays, the way he decorates his shop walls, and the design of his instruments. A "systemic interrelationship" links Milan's personal experience narratives with other forms of his individual and cultural expressions, which transcends the individual telling of a story or creative act (Bauman 1987:198).

The first theme that emerges from Milan's story is that he focuses his narrative on those who helped or encouraged him, a practice that reflects his deep appreciation for the support of the family and friends who backed his talents. For example, his brother the hunter, his neighbor the butcher, and his mother the cook all play prominent roles in the story, even though some listeners might construe their participation in the making of the prima as secondary. In fact, the tale centers on his family rather than his craftsmanship. His story of making his first instrument contains very little about the actual making of the instrument, but relates finding the prima with the help of his family.

Milan's free exchange of the word "prima" for "turtle" is an effective narrative device, which he does in both his earlier summarized story and this longer iteration. The turtle is the prima in earnest. While a turtle is an animal, a prima is a thing. Nevertheless, with its "churning" legs and "walking" corpse, the narrated turtle does not easily morph from the animate to the inanimate. It took the special skill of his mother to transform the animal into food, just as Milan would convert the shell into an instrument. Skill, talent, and other forms of specialized knowledge are transformative resources in Milan's stories, capable of changing plywood and rubber bands into an instrument, an animal into food, and a turtle into a prima. In addition, just as his father was a "craftsman in his own right," Milan's brother is an "expert marksman." Talent and skill are abundant in his narrated family.

Finally, the turtle story ends not in complete success, but in measured achievement that inspired future attempts, just as in the story of the plywood prima, where Milan's father "created [his] desire" to build instruments, and in the Hlad prima story that put "a little bug in" Milan to become a builder. A third theme, then, and perhaps the main point of the turtle story, is that measured success fosters future accomplishments, which is an important narrative in the workshop where Milan has taught literally hundreds of instrument builders. Each of these themes is a life lesson that the storyteller aims to impart to his audience, and his display provides the material evidence to support his story.

Lene Otto and Lykke Pendersen observed that older adults can use personal objects as the material artifacts of a life lived, markers of personal accomplishments, and evidence of problems solved (1998:88). In many ways, Milan's turtleback prima holds a special place in his personal archive of possessions, not because of its craftsmanship or tonal qualities, but rather because of the narrative that the elder has constructed around it. Though common from the late-nineteenth through the mid-twentieth century, primas crafted from turtle shells have now nearly vanished from production due to the endangerment of most varieties of turtles globally. Milan made his first prima from the shell of an Indiana "swamp" turtle, which the maker later realized was the wrong variety for building instruments.[11] Constructed more than half a century ago, Milan's first instrument is attractive, but it represents the work of a novice.[12] Despite his age, the decorative bračs, bugarias, and primas that he builds today far surpass his first attempt, which has an unbalanced shape and a dull tone. Nevertheless, he proudly displays his first effort as artifactual proof of his life story and material evidence of persistent personal themes to the elder.

When placed alongside Ivan Hlad's turtleback prima, the formal antecedents of Milan's first instrument become apparent. Both primas have the same distinctive, decorative, violin-style scrolls and employ the same headstock design that conceals the machine pegs under a screwed-on metal plate.[13] Although the two instruments differ in tone and scratchboard pattern, as well as in more subtle elements of design, the similarity in concept, form, and visual aesthetic is apparent. Milan says, "I patterned a lot of things after what he did, because I thought so much of him as a builder."

Along with the decorative scroll, both builders employed a six-string peg head, which is significant in this Serbo-Croatian instrument. Traditionally, primas have either five or six strings, and the number tends to divide along ethnic boundaries: Serbians favor the five-string primas, Croatians prefer six strings. Milan explains:

> Whenever I get an order for an instrument, and they tell me that they want a six-string instrument, versus a five-string instrument, I can tell you their nationality. Because the Croatian folks like the double set of wires, where the Serbians only use a double on the first and a single on the second. And through the years [Milan shakes his head] . . . never a mistake, it's always the same; I can tell you the nationality by the way they order that instrument.

As I noted before, Milan copied the Hlad instrument, which included making it a six-string instrument. However, even though Milan's instrument was built as a six-string, Hlad set it up and strung it with only five strings, which makes it sound and play in a traditional Serbian aesthetic. It is noteworthy that Milan's main instrument that he plays today is a five-string prima with a scroll headstock, even though his early exposure to the object was in the six-string Croatian form. Milan was born into an ethnically blended family and abhors the discordant split that he has witnessed between the Serbs and the Croats, but in many ways self-identifies as Serbian. He has a Serbian name, his wife is Serbian, they go to St. Sava Serbian Orthodox Church, and he writes for *Serb World USA*, a quarterly publication about Serbian culture and history. In this light, setting up a six-string prima to play like a five-string seems perfectly in keeping with his blended Serbian and Croatian identity.

Milan's shop is a place where he tells stories and makes instruments. Having listened to his stories and looked closely at the images and the instrument, the meaning of this life-story display comes into sharper focus. The pictures and the prima reference an often-told story and its related materials, opening up a space where the teller can share his stories, meanings can emerge, and the self is stated and sustained. What once were pictures of a man with a turtle, a married couple, and an instrument maker, now triangulate with an old instrument hanging on the wall and reference a series of stories that evoke the personal and cultural identity of the storyteller. His shop becomes a place not just for building and repairing instruments but a site for sharing stories, through which the artisan can build and repair his community.

It was on that day in Milan's workshop when I asked about the turtle picture that I began to understand the significance of his life-story display. I looked around the shop; I saw other photographs of builders, snapshots of musicians, and old instruments hanging on the walls. I heard the hum of the old Delta drill press that once belonged to Hlad, and saw Milan working on a new prima. I noticed other clusters of objects all around me and realized that I did not know all the stories that accompany them. However, the narrative I traced centers on a prima made by a young Serbo-Croatian musician who was inspired to build a turtleback prima. With the help of family and by copying instruments he had seen other places, he made one. It was "not much on sound, but it was an incentive to go ahead and make a number two instrument."

Epilogue

Milan Opacich departed this life on January 20, 2013. Though folklorists had worked with him for nearly forty years, and he was eighty-four years old, many in his home community and beyond commented that it was a life cut too short.

I had invited the instrument maker to accompany me to Washington, DC, to demonstrate his craft and talk about his life and the many Indiana University folklore students with whom he worked over the decades. But a week before he was to be at the 2012 Smithsonian Folklife Festival, he was admitted to the hospital. He had pancreatic cancer.

As soon as I returned from DC, my wife, son, and I went to see my friend. This visit was different from all of the previous times I had been to see him. I rarely recorded my conversations with Milan because his life had been documented so much; often we would just visit as friends. This time, he wanted me to record his stories one last time.

I realized that all the other tellings of his stories were rehearsals for this visit.

For nearly an hour and a half after I turned on my recorder, Milan talked and performed. He was not just speaking to me, but to future generations who would listen to his stories about his life as luthier, musician, and fireman. The avid historian was performing his story, and he knew it. Yet he was not pedantic or self-aggrandizing, but rather he spoke in his practiced style—humble and articulate. He told tight stories that flowed one to the next, as one can do only with a well-honed style. I rarely prompted or interrupted his stream of stories; my presence was less as a folklorist and more as a documentarian. He spoke of his trials as a fireman, the visits with Richard Dorson and the Gary Gang, and in general, what he called his "wonderful life."

In December 2012, just after completing my written doctoral exams, I visited Milan for the last time. The storyteller, who was always bigger than life, had lost fifty pounds and had grown frail. Between visitors and naps, he spent his days organizing the ephemera that had once filled the walls and boxes in his workshop. Now arranged into binders, Milan would refer to these materials to invoke his stories. Again, he wanted me to record him; this time his spirit was willing but his body was weak. Nevertheless, he pushed himself toward performance. He told me of the one-string gusle he owned that he believed once belonged to the famous epic poet and bard Petar Perunovic. He spoke of uncovering the forgotten story of Andrew Greochel, the tamburitza maker and founder of Kay Guitars, which Milan turned into an article for *Serb World USA*. As he began to lose steam, I asked him one last time to tell me the story of the turtleback prima. With a wry smile, he reflected, "I've gotten a lot of miles out of that one." He began his story, but soon lost his way, digressing into other related anecdotes and observations. I had hoped to have one last version of this story he had told so often.

Later, we moved into his living room, where atop the baby grand piano, the maker displayed several special instruments: the prima built on the National Mall in 1976; his personal instrument with beautiful chip-carving and amazing tone; and the turtleback prima, which had been moved there when Milan dismantled his workshop weeks earlier. While he told me about the instruments, the doorbell rang. I answered the door; there stood a young couple from St. Sava Church who had stopped by to visit Milan. In the entryway, we all spoke; the dog barked; the phone rang; but when the husband saw the instrument made from a swamp turtle, he asked Milan if he had made it. The old storyteller, tired from his day of visitors, summarized the story one last time. The confusion of the moment melted away as he spoke once more of turtle hunting, soup making, and instrument building.

Notes

1. Milan is widely considered the lay historian for the Serbian community in the greater Gary area. His workshop is a place that bustles with visitors, who stop to talk about music and local history. Throughout his conversations with visitors, he often references the objects and photographs on his workshop walls.

2. These exhibits are examples of what Barbara Kirshenblatt-Gimblett refers to as "ensembles" and Jack Santino calls "assemblage," which are creative displays that result from the "combining of a variety of symbolic elements within a single frame and the creation of a single aesthetic entity by grouping together disparate things" (Kirshenblatt-Gimblett 1985:333; Santino 1992:160). Kirshenblatt-Gimblett explains that "collections create their own frame of reference," and offer older adults "the pleasures of control, order, and relative closure within a hermetic universe" (1985:332). Henry Glassie also writes about objects collected and displayed in his *Passing the Time in Ballymenone*, where Ellen Cutler artfully displays her dishes on her dresser in her home (1982:61, 241).

3. Used interchangeably with tambura, tamburitza refers to a class of South Slavic fretted stringed instruments. Richard March notes that these instruments "range in size from smaller than a mandolin to larger than a string bass . . . The smallest instrument, the *prima*, is usually oval-shaped, while the medium-range instruments, *brač*, *čello brač*, and *bugarija*, most often have guitar-shaped sound boxes. The largest instrument in the family, the *berde*, is rarely used today" (1977:127).

4. For examples see March 1977, Dorson 1981, Eckstien 2004.

5. The prima is the treble instrument in a tamburitza orchestra, often tuned to the keys of D, G, or E. It is loosely related to a mandolin.

6. Although "Serbo-Croatian" is a problematic term both historically and politically, I employ it here because it is the term Milan uses to refer to his cultural identity.

7. In other versions of this story, Milan states that the homemade instrument was a ukulele rather than a prima.

8. For more about Frank Valentich and his instruments see Doris Dyen's 1988 essay.

9. In some versions of the story, the swamp is in Michigan City.

10. *The Birth of a Prima*. In *Crafting Sound: Indiana Instrument Makers* (DVD). Traditional Arts Indiana (2007).

11. In subsequent years, the luthier used gopher tortoise shells that a friend in Florida would send him, but today the gopher tortoise is a federally listed endangered species, and the changes in laws and growing conservation awareness has ended the making of instruments from turtle shells in the United States and Europe. Milan explains, "Turtles in our country are on the endangered list. You dare not hunt them now . . . so you don't get any [primas] made out of turtle shells anymore."

12. As noted in the analysis of the turtle narrative, Milan's story about making his first prima is really a story about his family and the hunting and eating of the turtle. Nevertheless, when pressed about the actual making of the object, Milan recalls additional details and short narratives. Milan purchased the straight-grained Sitka spruce top on that first prima from Ivan Hlad's son, Louie, who was also a Chicago luthier. For the scratchboard, a traditional type of "pick guard" that keeps plectrums from scratching the soft spruce top, Milan inlaid a thin but highly figured sheet of Brazilian rosewood veneer. He drilled four sets of holes in cross patterns into the top; however, the holes seem off center. (He later used a template to plot his tone-hole placement and pattern to ensure that the instrument looks symmetrical, but it is obvious that the novice arranged them by eye.) Once he drilled the holes, he seared them with a hot poker to seal the wood and make the pattern contrast from the blond wood top. Milan made his first prima neck from mahogany with a rosewood fingerboard, which he attached to the body with a dovetail joint.

13. The flat headstock, which terminates into a violin-style scroll, is strikingly similar to Hlad's instrument. Milan's scroll copies Hlad's in shape and size, though Hlad's has a sharper carving style and smoother finish. Milan made a few primas with a scroll in his later life, but his scrolls have evolved over the years to be smaller, lighter, and more finely carved.

Conclusion: Life-Story Objects and Aging in Indiana

When an old person tells a story about his or her own life, he is not only
projecting an identity, he is engaging a listener in the sharing of a ritual, thus
attempting to project continuity into the future through that listener.

(Mullen 1992:278)

OFTEN CONCEIVED AS a natural decline into a state of fragility, forgetfulness,
and isolation, aging in America is frequently understood as the inevitable decline
that all who live long enough will face. However, gerontologists, therapists, and
advocates now recognize that growing old does not have to be seen as an even-
tual failure, but rather an important developmental stage that can be accomplished (Erikson 1950; 1997).[1] Gene Cohen recommended that rather than only
acknowledging the adversity that accompanies the aging process, older adults
(and scholars) should recognize the great human potential that comes with
advanced years (Cohen 2005). Indeed, as these pages have revealed, some seniors
tap into their creative and personal potential through making life-story objects,
which helps them not only cope with the ails of aging, but also achieve greater
satisfaction with their lives.

Beyond life-story objects, there are other expressive acts and narrative projects that elders embrace to aid them in aging and reaching their creative potential. Otis Todd hosts weekly jams at his home in Brown County; through playing
old-time country and bluegrass music, he attracts younger musicians to whom he
tells his stories and teaches his repertoire. My grandmother, Mabel Kay, cooked
well into her eighties, and relished telling her grandchildren about hog butcher-
ing and canning as we sat down to our Sunday dinner. Although playing music,
cooking, and storytelling can be closely related creative activities to the artistic pursuits presented, I have chosen to narrow my focus to life-story objects,
because they remain an understudied but persistent aspect in the creative lives of
some older adults.

The more I pursue life-story objects, the more instances I find of elders who
recall and remake their world through the items they create and the stories they
tell through them. For example, Elmer Schlensker grew up helping his father make

brooms. As a boy, Elmer never made a complete broom by himself. However, in his retirement years, the senior took several of his father's old brooms apart to remind him how they were put together; through trial and error, he taught himself the craft (figure 6.1). Up until his death in 2012, Elmer enjoyed demonstrating broommaking each year at the Lanesville Festival, where he told people about his family tradition. Moreover, he often bragged that five generations of his family had made brooms, having taught both his daughter and grandson the local craft. Whether revived from childhood memories or inspired by their capacity to connect elders to others, meaningful memory projects serve as a lens for focusing on the long ago and sharing distant memories. These undertakings are rooted in the past, yet they propel themselves into the future through acts of creation,

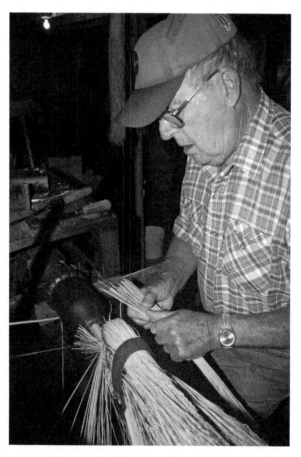

Fig. 6.1 Elmer Schlensker making a broom in his
basement in Millport, Indiana, 2009.

demonstration, exhibition, and/or narration. Although some life-story objects, like Elmer's brooms, are associated with past ways of life or a family tradition, the creations presented in the preceding chapters go further in that they visually and/or symbolically reference specific stories, people, and places.

The artists visited in this book point toward ways that elders strive for satisfaction and purpose in their lives through art and story. Using the arts in eldercare has become common over the last thirty years, and now clinical therapies that encourage reminiscence are routine; however, further research into vernacular forms of material life review is needed.[2] I offer this book as one model for studying this phenomenon. It includes examples of older adults who deploy their memory projects to deal with the difficulties of aging, such as feelings of isolation, loneliness, boredom, and uselessness.[3] While their art helps communicate personal stories, it is also transformative—often productively redefining, punctuating, and summing up the elder's life.

My performance-centered approach has relied heavily on the ethnographic observation of older adults making, using, and narrating their creations in context, which is why I have focused exclusively on contemporary folk artists. While I believe life-story objects probably represent a widespread and age-old genre, there is little data on the everyday creative lives of seniors from the past. Making grand pronouncements about geographic distribution and historical instances of material forms of life review are beyond the scope of this book; nevertheless, I am sure that throughout the twentieth century, many older adults made life-story objects in their later years.[4]

One historic example from Indiana is George L. Lucas (1856–193?), who worked for more than fifty years building and repairing railroad cars.[5] When he retired from the Baltimore & Ohio Railroad in 1927 at the age of seventy, he began making miniatures of the engines and cars he once produced. Over the years, he gave some of his creations to his grandson as birthday presents, including a passenger coach, a boxcar, and an engine and coal car. He made them accurate in "appearance and in proportions," including painstakingly equipping them with air brakes and automatic couplers. It took the elder at least a month to make each of his miniature railroad cars, a time investment Lucas enjoyed. An *Indianapolis Sunday Star* article noted, "To Mr. Lucas's way of thinking there is no better way of spending a wintry evening than this small-scale construction work, while he is located conveniently and comfortably close to the stove" (May 5, 1929, p. 41). Although it is impossible to know the narrative and interactional aspects of Lucas's creations, this brief profile reveals many of the same traits exhibited by the artists in this book. The train builder usually worked when he was alone; employed materials that were significant to his personal history, cultural identity, and/or social situation; started making his art after he retired; invested long periods of time in designing and making his work; and used his creations to make meaningful connections with others. Though this list of traits outlines some common denominators in the life-story work of older adults, it also contrasts with many of the common practices employed in reminiscence and art therapies today.

Working in Isolation

Like George Lucas, Bob, Gus, John, Marian, and Milan dedicate long periods of time in reflection and creation of their story objects, with winter often being an especially productive time. Spending days, weeks, and even months working on these personal objects provide elders with a special task to which they can devote themselves. What was Lucas thinking as he made his miniature trains? Perhaps he contemplated his years of service to the railroad or the years he spent mastering his skill in building, designing, and repairing train cars.[6] A form of material life review, the time these seniors devote to planning and making their art helps them construct meaningful narratives out of disparate memories. However, gerontology has not always viewed reminiscence as a healthy and productive activity.

Gerontologist Robert Butler's 1963 article "The Life Review" challenged prevailing notions about the role of reminiscences in the lives of older adults. Unlike the writings of other gerontologists of the time who presumed that the habitual reflection on the past was dysfunctional, Butler argued that reviewing one's life is a "naturally occurring, universal mental process." He suggested the "realization of approaching dissolution and death, and the inability to maintain one's sense of personal invulnerability" encourages this practice (Butler 1963:66, 67). In addition, he proposed that this reflective process is potentially productive for seniors and allows them to recall, reorganize, and revise their understanding of experiences.

> As the past marches in review, it is surveyed, observed and reflected upon by the ego. Reconsideration of previous experiences and their meanings occurs, often with concomitant revised or expanded understanding. Such reorganization of past experiences may provide a more valid picture, giving new and significant meaning to one's life; it may also prepare one for death mitigating one's fears. (Butler 1963:68)

According to Butler, with an explanatory examination of the past, elders forge new meaning out of old memories, sometimes as a way to understand and perhaps come to terms with their personal history.

As in this book, some older adults manifest this reconsideration of the past in a markedly material way, which often increases the amount of time the elders spend in contemplation and creation (Barrett 1985:43–45). In addition, if there is a material product from their reminiscence, they may feel more at ease with the hours, days, and months they spend in their life review practice. These time-filling activities often help seniors productively fill the hours after they have raised their children, retired from their jobs, and/or lost a loved one.

Creative-aging workshops and programs that facilitate arts activities for older adults have become commonplace at senior centers and assisted-living facilities. However, in light of the large amount of time that the elders in this study spend in contemplation and creation, one questions the basic structure of these programs. Seniors would need to have access to materials and space throughout daytime and evening hours. John and Gus often worked in the evening, when they could not sleep and their memories and creative energies surged. In addition, many arts and aging programs are structured as workshops, where older adults gather to make art. However, for all of the seniors I spoke with, art is a solitary act. The elder creates while they are alone, and they share the art and the stories that go with it only after it is completed. This is not to say that art classes do not have their place or value, but rather it suggests that gerontologists and arts professionals should look to vernacular forms of material life review to learn how to better structure and augment their offerings to older adults.

Significance of Media

An artist could select almost any medium to make their life-story objects, yet often the materials they choose hold some significance in their life or community. Lucas constructed trains from iron, tin, and wood, perhaps because that is what he used to build and repair full-size trains. Furthermore, he used "standard railroad paints" in the manufacture of his miniature cars and engines, making them as accurate in detail as possible. One could imagine that the senior was familiar with using these materials, after his years of working on trains, and these real railroad colors made his memory objects faithful in appearance. The materials chosen by each elder in my survey were determined in part by each maker's personal history, cultural identity, or current social context.

From whittling neckerchief slides as a kid, to carving models as a professional patternmaker, woodcarving is a defining part of Bob's life. Choosing to *carve* his life-story objects in wood goes beyond mere familiarity or access to the material; he has selected a medium that reflects his personal, family, and occupational identities. Like the grain running through his woodcarvings, Bob's message and material are tightly bound. Each panel communicates part of the maker's story visually and materially, before he ever speaks. Likewise, John's selection of a walking stick to tell his story of Ada and the general store was a natural choice. Since his youth, he has carried a stick on his walks. Moreover, the portability of the cane made his tale easily transportable and tellable. Like all storytelling events, there is a close relationship between the story being told and the way in which it is communicated; perhaps this is even more so for material forms of narratives.

Where Bob's and John's media of choice were rooted in their childhood, Marian and Gus chose their art forms later in life, and their materials have little to do with their personal history. Marian was always artistic and did handwork throughout her life, but hooking rugs is relatively new to her—she started in 2005. Nevertheless, the medium is significant, not because of how long she has done it, but because it connects her to a local community of rug hookers. Where she could have chosen needlepoint or some other art form, making rugs was her entrée into a community of hookers. Gus did not start painting until he retired. His medium is not tied to tradition, education, or any specific community of painters, but rather to the museum where he exhibits his works. His medium of choice is practical and functional for his social needs. His flat paintings hang on walls, waiting for narration. Comparably, Milan's photographic display was situationally appropriate. It exists in an opportune location where his students and customers entered his workshop. Life-story objects must work in culturally, socially, and contextually suitable ways in order to be effective, and this impacts the appropriateness of the material used by each elder.

Counselors seeking to find successful art therapies for older adults should be aware of these cultural, social, and practical aspects of material forms of life review. In his insightful essay on the relationship between folklife and aging, Alan Jabbour recognized that the expressive works of seniors reflect "individual needs and personalities" as well as cultural heritage and habits. He cautioned against wholesale approaches to arts-in-aging work:

> But we must be cautious here. Not just any folk art will do. The old woman in a Norwegian community in Kansas may have a tradition of fashioning exquisitely crafted woven hotpads or potholders, but it does not follow that we should set about mobilizing every rest home in the country toward the production of potholders. Nor do all old people need a little fiddle music on Saturday night to uplift their spirits and fire their imaginations. (Jabbour 1981:143)

Just as an older adult's medical prescriptions are particular to their physical needs, the art practices of elders are based upon on a variety of cultural, social, and personal factors.[7]

Retirement, Ritual, and Reflection

Lucas making miniatures in retirement is not unique. In fact, each of the elders presented in this study started their memory projects after they retired or when they experienced some other rupture in their daily lives. Marian started making rugs when she relocated to a new community and used the craft to make new friends at the rug-hooking club in Chesterton. Once retired, Milan created his display at the entrance to his workshop after his brother died, so he could tell his students about his brother and the making of the prima. Similarly, John started decorating his walking sticks after he sold the store and his wife passed away. Like the others, Gustav and Bob started their memory projects after they left their jobs. Why is retirement a major catalyst for making life-story objects? Though it might be that after leaving the workforce, seniors had time to make art, other factors are also at play (Barrett 1985:39, 45).

A ritualized event that marks a person's transition from worker to retiree, retirement is a rite of passage. Arnold Van Gennep observed that there is an essential underlying structure to all rites of passage, from baptisms to bar mitzvahs. His three-phase model progresses from a time of separation through a transitional state, and finally to reincorporation into a new role or status (Van Gennep 1909; Turner 1969). Perhaps the most recognizable rite of passage in the United States is the transition of two people from being engaged to being married, with new roles and responsibilities. Through rites of passages, a bride becomes a wife, a boy changes to a man, or a sinner converts to a saint. Each of these new roles brings new expectations and obligations. However, Peter Jarvis, using Van Gennep's conception of rites of passage, rightly explains that retirement in the United States is an incomplete passage. Retiring seniors go through the predictable time of "separation" that Van Gennep identified, but it is not followed by a process of "incorporation." There is no formalized way for elders to transition into their new role as a retiree. Moreover, there is no defined role or expectation for these older adults (Jarvis 1989). This might be why some seniors flounder after leaving the workforce: they remain in a liminal state, unprepared for their new post-work lives.

As anthropologist Barbara Myerhoff has observed, beyond the fiftieth wedding anniversary, milestone birthdays, and retirement celebrations, there is a scarcity of recognized societal rituals in later life. However, some elders have developed their own private or personal rituals to mark the passage of time and reflect upon and assign meaning to aspects of their lives. Ritualized activities, such as the art projects presented, have helped older adults navigate losing a spouse, selling the family home, and retiring from a career (Myerhoff 1984b:308, 311).

In making art, the elders featured in this book have developed a ritual practice that has helped them to thrive in their retirement years. Through these creative practices, they forged new identities for themselves: Bob Taylor, the carver of memories; Gus Potthoff, the memory painter; Marian Sykes, the rug hooker; John Schoolman, the cane man; and Milan Opacich, the instrument maker and storyteller. More than mere time-filling activities for the retirees, these undertakings allowed the seniors to adopt new roles that redefined them. Their new identities, however, did not erase their past lives, but built upon them—new lives that include sharing scenes and stories from their past.

Through making their life-story art, Bob, Gus, John, Marian, and Milan transitioned past mere retirement.

As discussed, older adults must learn to adapt to their new, post-retirement life. After his wife passed, John devoted hours to making his walking sticks and other art projects. The time he spent contemplating and making canes helped fill the hours he spent at home alone, but also furnished him with conversation pieces to help him interact with others when he went to the Senior PrimeLife Enrichment Center or on one of his other outings or walks. The relationship between making life-story objects and retirement is both expressive and instrumental in the lives of elders. These special creations are often coping strategies that aid retirees in negotiating this new stage of life.

When Gus talks about his museum volunteering and late-night painting, he often refers to these activities as his "work." His art making, a type of personal, ritual practice, not only occupies his day and evening hours, but also provides him with a strong sense of purpose and pride. Each of the elders profiled similarly use their art and narrative undertakings as new vocations. Their new work has helped them navigate a difficult rite of passage and provided them with the skills and tools needed for this new chapter in their lives.

Meaningful Connections

One product of engaging in these adaptive pursuits is that elders are able to form and maintain personal relationships. Whether exhibiting or giving away a life-story object, artists engage in a special kind of communicative conduct that often involves others. Lucas used his art to form a bond with his grandson by giving him his homemade trains; in fact, they shared a love of trains.[8] In addition, the senior probably shared his handiwork with others through explanations and stories. The artists presented in the preceding chapters use their works to connect and relate to others in a variety of ways. While some make works explicitly to be gifts or presentational pieces, others construct their items to serve as props for stories, illustrations of how things use to be, and material appeals for narrative encounters. Nevertheless, each endowed their objects with the capacity to express a relationship or impart meaning to the receiver or audience. Scholars such as Michael Owen Jones and Simon Bronner demonstrate that researchers should not just look at the maker but also recognize the role of receivers/audience in shaping the creation and performance of things (Jones 1989; Bronner 1996:105–116).

One winter, I spent several days with Milan, and he helped me build a guitar. While there, I witnessed how the display that referenced the story of his first prima worked to forge a connection with instrument-making students. The display and its story of encouragement and perseverance were created with the novice in mind. Though Milan was now a master builder, he used the narrative of his humble beginnings to connect with and inspire dozens of instrument-making students.

As much of this book has demonstrated, seniors make and/or display many of their objects to tell stories. They create paintings, carvings, rugs, canes, and displays for narrative encounters. Using their creations, elders connect with others as storytellers, relating meaningful experiences through words and art. Life-story objects help their creators connect to their audience, whether it be a family member, friend, caregiver, student, or folklorist, their art attracts attention and facilitates social interactions. Through these items, they can summon whole worlds—explaining how things used to be, describing relationships with friends and families, and relating details about special events and places. The union of words and objects in performance links elders to their listeners, fulfilling an overt function of these curious creations. John Rowe and Robert Kahn argued that maintaining personal relationships and engaging in productive activities, as each of the people profiled have done, are central aspects of what they viewed as "successful aging" (Rowe and Kahn 1998).[9] Through creation and narration, the seniors strive to remain socially engaged.

Gifting these types of items often initiates a complex system of affiliation and expectations between the giver and the recipient (Mauss 1954). The elder communicates the stories and ideas invested in the objects, aiming to form a personal connection with the receiver, hoping that the gift will carry the story forward and be shared with others. Like an oddly benevolent Trojan horse, these handmade gifts hold more than what the beneficiary may realize. Within these objects are hidden obligations and expectancies owed to their maker.

Most of Gus's images in the Atterbury-Bakalar Museum are scenes he painted expressly to tell specific stories; however, each year he also creates hundreds of paintings of building the Thailand-Burma Railway that he offers to others as gifts with the expectation that the recipients will carry his story forward and tell it to others who see his painting. Through both the narrative and exchange uses of his creations, Gus forges personal bonds with others. After my first meeting with the artist, he made me three small paintings on muslin, each recording a different aspect of the Death Railway. After receiving the generous gift, I felt compelled to tell his story to others, which on some unspoken level the artist required of me. Though in his nineties, he continues to create paintings for museums, schools, veterans, and others.

John did not plan to part with most of his sticks, but he made several explicitly to give away. The family-tree canes, sticks that record a friend's genealogy, were clearly made as gifts for special friends. He also commonly presented sticks to veterans as a way to thank them for their service and relate with them as a fellow veteran. Occasionally, if someone expressed special interest in one of his sticks, John would give it to them or make them another in the style of the first. Barb Hetrick, who worked at SPEC, received several sticks from the senior this way. These gifted sticks are less about transmitting information and more about expressing his appreciation for who they are or what they have done. Although Milan gave his first prima away, he regretted it and was thrilled when it returned to him. Gifting items, though common among older adults who create art, is not universal. Marian has every rug she ever made, even though several friends and family members have asked for one. For her, parting with a rug would be like losing a part of her past. Similarly, Bob never wanted to part with one of his memory carvings. He only consented to let go of his St. John's Church carving because it was going to the church.

In addition to narrating and gifting items to build and maintain relationships, artists can use their creations to connect with people from the past. Gus paints to remember his comrades, especially an Australian friend he buried in a shallow grave. Milan built his display to recall family, particularly his "dearly departed brother." Marian makes rugs, often to connect with memories of when her children were at an ideal age. "When they were little" and she "could be with them," before "they grew older, and went their way." John's general store stick recalls not just his wife Ada, but summons a whole community of people erased by time. In another stick that John made, he lists the people who lived in Bippus, back when they had the store. One can imagine the time he spent recalling names, and the memories of people who came into his life. Henry Glassie refers to these associations as "connections built in the mind" (1989:236). Much like how seniors deploy their art to initiate and facilitate social interactions, they also use the time they spend designing and making their projects to reconnect with the past. Whether recalling particular people or whole communities, these works bring the forgotten back to mind and give material substance to fleeting social bonds often erased by time.

Like the painted icons in the Serbian Orthodox church, Milan's display of photographs brought to mind important people who shaped his life and whom he enjoyed recalling. As he was dying of cancer, he spoke even more of his mother, father, and brother. He spent the last few months of his life organizing the collection of images and newspaper clippings that had once adorned his shop walls. He did this in part to leave a legacy through the binders he assembled, but also to recall his past and relive (or reconnect with) memories of his family, tamburitza musicians, and others who touched his life. Making life-story objects not only helps seniors relate to people socially, they assist them in conjuring a complete cast of characters through reminiscence and storytelling.

These special objects help form one additional connection in the lives of elders—a reconnection of self. Henry Glassie, in *The Spirit of Folk Art*, writes about Lou Sesher, a retired riverman who made models of boats he recalled from his youth. Glassie observed that Sesher's miniature boats were "communications with himself about himself" and were material manifestations of memories that "bore the potential for making connections with others" (Glassie 1989:236). Connecting one's past with one's current state and sharing insights and narratives with others are part of what Gene Cohen and others have recognized as the "summing up" phase of one's life, often typified by reviewing, summarizing, and giving back to others (Cohen 2005:75–82).

It seems appropriate to conclude with the "summing up" aspects of folk art in aging. More than just about recalling one's personal history, making life-story objects help some elders make sense out of that past. Using Erik Erikson's theory of "ego integration," it seems that many seniors use their special art projects to cultivate a "meaningful interplay between" their earlier life and their later years and in doing so they develop a "sense of summary" for their lives through their memory art (Erikson 1997:63).

Marian's Little Italy rug, Bob's Mission Festival carving, Gus's freedom painting, John's general store cane, and Milan's prima display are examples of the creative ways that elders can make their pasts a meaningful part of their later years while finding new purpose in their lives as creators and storytellers. The sum of their life's work is more than their artistic output. John made more than a thousand sticks and canes, Marian just hooked her nineteenth rug; it is impossible to know how many paintings Gus produced, but it would surely number well into the thousands. Nevertheless, the art made by these seniors is a beautiful byproduct of lives lived, thoughtfully recalled, and strategically shared to alleviate some of the physical, social, and psychological ills that beset so many of their generation.

Notes

1. Erik Erikson first postulated that there are developmental stages that must be accomplished throughout one's lifespan. It was upon this concept that Robert Butler hinged his assessment of life review as a "naturally occurring, universal mental process" or stage that is "characterized by the progressive return to consciousness of past experiences" (Butler 1963:66).

2. North Dakota state folklorist Troyd Geist and a team of arts and senior-care professionals have developed an arts-in-eldercare initiative called the "Arts for Life Program." Their initiative addresses what geriatric physician Dr. William Thomas calls "Three Plagues" that threaten the well-being of those in eldercare institutions: loneliness, boredom, and helplessness. The Arts for Life Program has brought quilters, potters, painters, and musicians into senior-care facilities to help address these ails. Their program has become a model arts-in-aging program. For more about this successful program, see the North Dakota Council on the Arts' *Art for Life: The Therapeutic Power and Promise of the Arts* (2003).

In addition, David Shuldiner (1949–2002) worked with the Connecticut Humanities Council as a scholar in residence. He developed a program using his skills as a folklorist to facilitate educational programs for older adults. For more information about the Connecticut program, see David Shuldiner's "Promoting Self-Worth among the Elderly" in *Putting Folklore to Use* (1994:214–225).

3. My research methods have roots in material behavior scholarship in folklore (Bauman 1969; Bronner 1981; 1996; Georges 1969; 1980; Jones 1997; 1993; 1989).

4. Didi Barrett contends that older adults beginning to make art is a phenomena that emerged in the twentieth century (1985:39).

5. Information about George L. Lucas is from an article in the *Indianapolis Sunday Star*, May 5, 1929, p. 41, and the 1920 and 1930 US Census.

6. Lucas received a patent for one of his designs (Patent Number: US792142).

7. When I presented a paper about John Schoolman at the 2012 American Folklore Society Annual Meeting, an attendee asked if I thought walking-stick workshops in senior centers might be a productive program. My response was that life-story objects are more complex than that. To be sure, it would be a fun activity for some, but stick making, or any other medium, is not universally significant in the lives of older adults.

8. The *Indianapolis Sunday Star* article noted that Lucas's young grandson, Myron Scarborough, spent much of his time drawing trains (41).

9. My approach runs parallel to the concept of "successful aging," which has gained widespread currency in gerontology (Havighurst 1961; Rowe and Kahn 1998). Predicated on positively addressing the issues that accompany aging, successful aging perspectives aim to holistically attend to a senior's physical, emotional, and social well-being and contend that older adults need to find satisfaction in/with their lives (Rowe and Kahn 1997 and 1998). Most scholars recognize that successful aging should remain a relative concept that takes into account cultural, social, and personal desires and expectations.

Bibliography

Allen, Barbara
  1998   Personal Experience Narratives: Use and Meaning In Interaction. *In* Folk
          Groups and Folklore Genres: A Reader. Elliott Oring, ed. Pp. 236–43. Logan:
          Utah State University Press.
Allport, Carolyn Jones, dir.
  1980   Sermons in Wood. 27 min. The Center for Southern Folklore. Memphis, TN.
Babcock, Barbara
  1986   Modeled Selves: Helen Cordero's "Little People." *In* The Anthropology of
          Experience. Victor Turner and Edward Bruner, eds. Pp. 316–43. Urbana:
          University of Illinois Press.
Babcock, Barbara A., Guy Monthan, and Doris Monthan.
  1986   The Pueblo Storyteller: Development of a Figurative Ceramic Tradition.
          Tucson: University of Arizona Press.
Barrett, Didi
  1985   A Time to Reap: Late Blooming Folk Artists. The Clarion 10(Fall):39–47.
Bauman, Richard
  1987   Ed Bell, Texas Storyteller: The Framing and Reframing of Life Experience.
          Journal of Folklore Research 24(3):197–221.
  1986   Story, Performance, and Event: Contextual Studies of Oral Narrative.
          Cambridge: Cambridge University Press.
  1969   Towards A Behavioral Theory of Folklore. Journal of American Folklore
          82(326):167–70.
Bauman, Richard, and Charles L. Briggs
  1990   Poetics and Performance as Critical Perspectives on Language and Social
          Life. Annual Review of Anthropology 19:59–88.
Beattie, Rod
  2009   The Death Railway: A Brief History of the Thailand-Burma Railway.
          Kanchanaburi, Thailand: TBRC Ltd.
Beck, Jane, ed.
  1988   Stories to Tell: The Narrative Impulse in Contemporary New England
          Folk Art. *In* Stories to Tell. Pp. 38–55. Lincoln, MA: De Cordova and Dana
          Museum and Park.
Ben Amos, Dan
  1972   Toward a Definition of Folklore in Context. *In* Toward New Perspectives
          in Folklore. Americo Parédes and Richard Bauman, eds. Pp. 3–15. Austin:
          University of Texas Press.
Bethke, Robert D.
  1996   Americana Crafted: Jehu Camper, Delaware Whittler. Jackson: University
          Press of Mississippi.

Bogatyrev, Petr
>   1971   The Functions of Folk Costume in Moravian Slovakia. Richard G. Crum, trans. The Hague: Mouton.

Bronner, Simon J.
>   2015   Forward: Folklore for the Ages. Midwestern Folklore 41(2): 3–7.
>   1996   [1985] The Carver's Art: Crafting Meaning from Wood. Lexington: University Press of Kentucky.
>   1992   Cane Making as Symbol and Tradition. *In* American Folk Art Canes: Personal Sculpture. George H. Meyer, ed. Pp. 219–21. Seattle: University of Washington Press.
>   1981   Investigating Identity and Expression in Folk Art. Winterthur Portfolio 16(1):65–83.

Burtscher, William John
>   1945   The Romance Behind Walking Canes. Philadelphia: Dorrance.

Bustin, Dillon
>   1988   Worlds of Folk Art. *In* Stories to Tell. Jane Beck, ed. Pp. 13–35. Lincoln, MA: De Cordova and Dana Museum and Park.

Bustin, Dillon, and Richard Kane, dirs.
>   1982   Water from Another Time. 28 min. Watertown, MA: Documentary Educational Resources.

Butler, Robert
>   1963   The Life Review: An Interpretation of Reminiscence in the Aged. Psychiatry 26(1):65–76.

Cardinal, Roger
>   2001   Memory Painting. *In* Self-Taught Art: The Culture and Aesthetics of American Vernacular Art. Charles Russell, ed. Pp. 95–116. Jackson: University Press of Mississippi.

Cashman, Ray, Tom Mould and Pravina Shukla
>   2011   The Individual and Tradition: Folkloristic Perspectives. Bloomington: Indiana University Press.

Cashman, Ray
>   2006   Critical Nostalgia and Material Culture in Northern Ireland. Journal of American Folklore 119(472):137–160.

Chapman, Sherry Ann
>   2006   A "New Materialist" Lens on Aging Well: Special Things in Later Life. Journal of Aging Studies 20(3): 207–16.

Chittenden, Varick A.
>   N.d.   Nostalgia: Re-Creating Memories. *In* Kindred Pursuits: Folk Art in North Country Life (online exhibition), http://folkart.tauny.org/nostalgia.html, accessed December 20, 2013.
>   1995   Vietnam Remembered: The Folk Art of Marine Combat Veteran Michael D. Cousino Sr. Jackson: University Press of Mississippi.
>   1989   "These Aren't Just My Scenes": Shared Memories in a Vietnam Veteran's Art. Journal of American Folklore 102(406):412–423.

Christensen, Danille Elise
>   2011   "Look at Us Now!": Scrapbooking, Regimes of Value, and the Risks of (Auto)Ethnography. Journal of American Folklore 124(493):175–210.

Cohen, Gene
  2006   Research on Creativity and Aging: The Positive Impact of the Arts on Health
         and Illness. Generations 30(1):7–15.
  2005   The Mature Mind: The Positive Power of the Aging Brain. New York: Basic
         Books.
  2000   The Creative Age: Awakening Human Potential in the Second Half of Life.
         New York: Avon Books.
Congdon, Kristin G., and Tina Bucuvalas
  2006   Mario Sanchez. *In* Just Above the Water: Florida Folk Art. Pp. 214–17.
         Jackson: University Press of Mississippi.
Coulter, Barbara
  2008   The Wonderful World of Marian Sykes: A Gallery of Memories. ATHA
         Newsletter 173(November):42–47.
de Queiroz, Chizuko Judy Sugita
  2004   Camp Days 1942–1945: Japanese American Internment Camps WWII. Los
         Angeles: Self-Published.
Dolby, Sandra Stahl
  1989   Literary Folkloristics and the Personal Narrative. Bloomington: Indiana
         University Press.
Dorson, Richard M.
  1981   Land of the Millrats. Cambridge: Harvard University Press.
Dow, James R.
  1970   The Hand Carved Walking Canes of William Baurichter. Keystone Folklore
         Quarterly 15(3):138–147.
Dusselier, Jane E.
  2008   Artifacts of Loss: Crafting Survival in Japanese American Concentration
         Camps. New Brunswick, NJ: Rutgers University Press.
Dyen, Doris
  1988   Frank Valentich: Croatian Tamburitza Maker. *In* Craft & Community:
         Traditional Arts in Contemporary Society. Shalom D. Staub, ed. Pp. 57–62.
         Washington, American Folklore Society.
Eaton, Allen
  1952   Beauty Behind Barbed Wire: The Arts of the Japanese in Our War
         Relocation Camps. New York: Harper.
Eckstein, Mary, and Milan Opacich
  2004   2004 NEA Heritage Fellow Milan Opacich. http://arts.gov/honors/heritage/
         fellows/milan-opacich, accessed September 9, 2014.
Erhard, Doris Francis
  1983   "Everybody in my family has something from me": Older Cleveland Folk
         Artists (exhibition catalogue). Cleveland: Department of Aging.
Erikson, Erik
  1997   The Lifecycle Completed. New York: Norton.
  1950   Childhood and Society. New York: Norton.
Fenton, William
  1950   Roll Call of the Iroquois Chiefs: A Study of a Mnemonic Cane from the Six
         Nations Reserve. Washington: Smithsonian Institution and the Cranbrook
         Institute of Science.

Ferris, William
  1982   Local Color: A Sense of Place in Folk Art. New York: McGraw-Hill.
Garthwaite, Chester
  1990   Threshing Days: The Farm Paintings of Lavern Kammerude. Mount Horeb:
          Wisconsin Folk Museum.
Geist, Troyd, ed.
  2003   Art for Life: The Therapeutic Power and Promise of the Arts. Bismark, ND:
          North Dakota Council on the Arts.
Georges, Robert A.
  1980   Toward a Resolution of the Text/Context Controversy. Western Folklore
          39(1):34–40.
  1969   Toward an Understanding of Storytelling Events. Journal of American
          Folklore 82(326):313–28.
Glassie, Henry.
  2010   Prince Twins Seven-Seven: His Art, His Life in Nigeria, His Exile in
          America. Bloomington: Indiana University Press.
  1998   Art and Life in Bangladesh. Bloomington: Indiana University Press.
  1993   Turkish Traditional Arts Today. Bloomington: Indiana University Press.
  1989   The Spirit of Folk Art: The Girard Collection at the Museum of International
          Folk Art. New York: Harry N. Abrams.
  1982   Passing the Time in Ballymenone. Bloomington: Indiana University Press.
  1973   Structure and Function, Folklore and the Artifact. Semiotics 7(4):333–41.
  1972   Folk Art. *In* Folklore and Folklife: An Introduction. Richard M. Dorson, ed.
          Pp. 253–80. Chicago: University of Chicago Press.
  1968   Pattern in the Material Folk Culture of the Eastern United States.
          Philadelphia: University of Pennsylvania Press.
  1967   William Houck: Maker of Pounded Ash Adirondack Pack-Baskets. Keystone
          Folklore Quarterly 12(1):23–54.
Goffman, Erving
  1983   The Interaction Order: American Sociological Association, 1982 Presidential
          Address. American Sociological Review 48(1):1–17.
Goldstein, Kenneth S.
  1962   William Robbie: Folk Artist of the Buchan District, Aberdeenshire. *In*
          Folklore in Action. Horace P. Beck, ed. Pp. 101–11. Philadelphia: University of
          Pennsylvania Press.
Grider, Sylvia Ann, and Barbara Ann Allen.
  1974   Howard Taylor, Cane Maker and Handle Shaver. Indiana Folklore
          7(1-2):1–25.
Hackley, Larry
  1988   Sticks: Historical and Contemporary Kentucky Canes. Louisville: Kentucky
          Arts and Crafts Foundation.
Havighurst, Robert J.
  1961   Successful Aging. The Gerontologist 1(1):8–13.
Hayes, John P.
  1977   Mooney: The Life of the World's Master Carver. Midvale, OH: Dove
          Publishing Company.

Hirasuna, Delphine
    2005   The Art of Gaman: Arts and Crafts from the Japanese American Internment Camps, 1942–1946. New York: Ten Speed Press.
Hoskins, Janet
    1998   Biographical Objects: How Things Tell the Stories of People's Lives. New York: Routledge.
Hufford, Mary
    1984   All of Life's a Stage: The Aesthetics of Life Review. *In* 1984 Festival of American Folklife. Pp. 32–35. Washington: Smithsonian Institution and National Park Service.
Hufford, Mary, Marjorie Hunt, and Steven Zeitlin.
    1987   The Grand Generation: Memory, Mastery, Legacy. Washington: Smithsonian Institution.
Indianapolis Sunday Star
    1929   Fashions Two-foot Long Coaches, Engines at Home During Spare Time as Birthday Gifts for Grandson. May 5:41.
Jabbour, Alan
    1982   Some Thoughts from a Folk Cultural Perspective, *In* Perspectives on Aging, Priscilla W. Johnston, ed. Pp. 139–49. Cambridge: Ballinger Publishing Company.
Jakobson, Roman
    1960   Closing Statement: Linguistics and Poetics. *In* Style in Language. Thomas A. Sebeok, ed. Pp. 350–77. Cambridge: Massachusetts Institute of Technology Press.
Jarvis, Peter
    1989   Retirement: An Incomplete Ritual. Journal of Educational Gerontology 4(2):79–84.
Jones, Michael Owen
    2000   "Tradition" in Identity Discourses and an Individual's Symbolic Construction of Self. Western Folklore 59(2):115–141.
    1997   How Can We Apply Event Analysis to "Material Behavior," and Why Should We? Western Folklore 56(3–4):199–214.
    1995   The 1995 Archer Taylor Memorial Lecture. Why Make (Folk) Art? Western Folklore 54(4):253–276.
    1993   Why Take a Behavioral Approach to Folk Objects? *In* History from Things: Essays on Material Culture. Steven Lubar and W. David Kingery, eds. Pp. 182–96. Washington: Smithsonian Institution Press.
    1989   Craftsman of the Cumberland: Tradition and Creativity. Lexington: University Press of Kentucky.
Jones, Suzie, ed.
    1980   Webfoots and Bunchgrassers: Folk Art of the Oregon Country. Salem: Oregon Arts Commission.
Kallir, Jane
    1982   Grandma Moses: The Artist behind the Myth. New York: Artline.
Kallir, Jane and Roger Cardinal
    2001   Grandma Moses in the 21st Century. New Haven: Yale University Press.

Kaufman, Barbara Wahl, and Didi Barrett
  1985   A Time to Reap: Late Blooming Folk Artists. South Orange, NJ: Seton Hall
         University.
Kent, William Winthrop
  1971   The Hooked Rug. Detroit, MI: Tower Books.
Kilmer, Joyce
  1914   The House with Nobody in It. *In* Trees and Other Poems. New York: George
         H. Doran Company.
Kirshenblatt, Mayer and Barbara Kirshenblatt-Gimblett.
  2007   They Called Me Mayer July: Painted Memories of a Jewish Childhood in
         Poland before the Holocaust. Berkeley: University of California Press.
Kirshenblatt-Gimblett, Barbara.
  1989   Authoring Lives. Journal of Folklore Research 26(2):123–49.
  1988   Mistaken Dichotomies. Journal of American Folklore 101(400):140–55.
  1987   Introduction. *In* The Grand Generation: Memory, Mastery, Legacy. Mary
         Hufford, Marjorie Hunt, and Steven Zeitlin, eds. Washington: Smithsonian
         Institution.
  1985   Objects of Memory: Material Culture as Life Review. *In* Folk Groups and
         Folklore Genres: A Reader. Elliott Oring, ed. Pp. 329–38. Logan: Utah State
         University Press.
Kopp, Joel and Kate Kopp
  1995   American Hooked and Sewn Rugs: Folk Art Underfoot. Albuquerque:
         University of New Mexico Press.
Larson, Renya T. H., and Susan Perlstein
  2007   When Words Are Not Enough: Art-Based Methods of Reminiscence.
         In Transformational Reminiscence: Life Story Work. John A. Kunz and
         Florence Gray Soltys, eds. Pp. 123–39. New York: Springer.
Leary, James P.
  1990   Introduction. *In* Threshing Days: The Farm Paintings of Lavern
         Kammerude. Mount Horeb, WI: Wisconsin Folk Museum.
Lesh, Eben
  1922   Our Grocery Store Man. *In* Miles of Smiles. Eben Lesh, ed. Pp. 9–11.
         Huntington, IN: Barnhart Book Store.
Linde, Charlotte
  1993   Life Stories: the Creation of Coherence. New York: Oxford University Press.
March, Richard
  1977   The Tamburitza Tradition in the Calumet Region. Indiana Folklore
         10(2):127–138.
Martin, Charles, dir.
  1982   Stitching Memories: The Art of Ethel Mohamed. 22 min. Clinton, MS:
         Learning Resources Center.
Mauss, Marcel
  1954   [1925] The Gift: The Form and Reason for Exchange in Archaic Societies. Ian
         Cunnison, trans. Glencoe, IL: Free Press.
Mordoh, Alice Morrison
  1980   Two Woodcarvers: Jasper, Dubois County, Indiana. Indiana Folklore
         13(1–2):17–29.

Mullen, Patrick B.

    1993   The Grand Generation: Memory Mastery, Legacy by Mary Hufford; Marjorie Hunt; Steven Zeitlin (Book Review). Journal of American Folklore 106(421): 363–65.

    1992   Listening to Old Voices: Folklore, Life Stories, and the Elderly. Urbana: University of Illinois Press.

Myerhoff, Barbara

    1992   Remembered Lives: The Work of Ritual, Performance and Growing Older. Marc Kaminsky, ed. Ann Arbor: University of Michigan Press.

    1986   Life Not Death in Venice: Its Second Life. *In* The Anthropology of Experience. Victor W. Turner and Edward M. Bruner, eds. Pp. 261–86. Chicago: University of Illinois Press.

    1984a Life Not Death in Venice. *In* 1984 Festival of American Folklife, Pp. 36–38. Smithsonian Institution and National Park Service.

    1984b Rites and Signs of Ripening: The Intertwining of Ritual, Time, and Growing Older. *In* Age and Anthropological Theory. David I. Kertzer and Jennie Kieth, eds. Pp. 305–30. Ithaca: Cornell University Press.

    1980   Number Our Days: A Triumph of Continuity and Culture Among Jewish Old People in an Urban Ghetto. New York: Touchstone.

    1978   Life History among the Elderly: Performance, Visibility, and Remembering. *In* A Crack in the Mirror. Jay Ruby, ed. Pp. 99–117. Philadelphia: University of Pennsylvania Press.

Newell, William W., ed.

    1888   On the Field and Work of the Journal of American Folk-Lore. Journal of American Folklore 1(1):3–7.

Noyes, Dorothy

    2008   Humble Theory. Journal of Folklore Research 45(1):37–44.

Ochayon, Sheryl Silver

    2013   Commemoration in the Art of Holocaust Survivors. *In* E-Newsletter for Holocaust Educators. The International School for Holocaust Studies, Yad Vashem/The Holocaust Martyrs' and Heroes' Remembrance Authority. http://www1.yadvashem.org/yv/en/education/newsletter/26/main_article.asp

Otto, Lene and Lykke L. Pendersen

    1998   Collecting Oneself: Life Stories and Objects of Memory. Ethnologia Scandinavica 28(1):78–92.

Peterson, Sally

    1988   Translating Experience and Reading a Story Cloth. Journal of American Folklore 101(399):6–22.

Pocius, Gerald L.

    1979   Hooked Rugs in Newfoundland: The Representation of Social Structure in Design. Journal of American Folklore 92(365):273–84.

Proby, Kathryn H.

    1981   Mario Sanchez: Painter of Key West Memories. Key West, FL: Southernmost Press.

Roach, Susan

    1992   The Journey of David Allen: Transformations through Public Folklore. *In* Public Folklore. Nicholas R. Spitzer and Robert Baron, eds. Pp. 159–82. Washington: Smithsonian Institution Press.

Roberts, Norma J.
  1992 Elijah Pierce, Woodcarver. Columbus, OH: Columbus Museum of Art.
Rogan, Bjarne
  1998 Things with a History-and Other Possessions: Some Notes on Public and
        Private Aspects of Possession among Elderly People. Ethnologia Scandinavica
        28(1):93–107.
Rowe, John. W. and Robert L. Kahn
  1997 Successful Aging. The Gerontologist, 37(4):433–40.
  1998 Successful Aging. New York: Dell Publishing.
Santino, Jack,
  1992 The Folk *Assemblage* of Autumn: Tradition and Creativity in Halloween
        Folk Art. *In* Folk Art and Art Worlds. John Michael Vlach and Simon J.
        Bronner, eds. Pp. 151–69. Logan: Utah State University Press.
Sciorra, Joseph
  2011 Locating Memory: Longing, Place and Autobiography in Vincenzo Ancona's
        Sicilian Poetry. *In* Italian Folk: Vernacular Culture in Italian-American
        Lives. Joseph Sciorra, ed. Pp. 107–32. New York: Fordham University Press.
  1985 Reweaving the Past: Vincenzo Ancona's Telephone Wire Figures. The
        Clarion (Spring/Summer):48–53.
Shimomura, Roger
  2011 Shadows of Minidoka. Lawrence, KS: Lawrence Arts Center.
Shukla, Pravina
  2008 The Grace of Four Moons: Dress, Adornment and the Art of the Body in
        Modern India. Bloomington: Indiana University Press.
Shuldiner, David P.
  1997 Folklore, Culture, and Aging: A Research Guide. Westport, CT:
        Greenwood Press.
  1994 Promoting Self-Worth among the Elderly. *In* Putting Folklore to Use. Michael
        Owen Jones, ed. Pp. 214–25. Lexington: University Press of Kentucky.
St. John-Erickson, Mark
  2001 More Than A Little Whittling: Carvings' Depth Not Measured In Just
        Inches. The Hampton Roads Daily Press, December 02. Hampton Roads:
        http://articles.dailypress.com/2001-12-02/entertainment/0111290423_1
        _carvings-camps-curio, accessed September 9, 2014.
Staudinger, Ursula M.
  2001 Life Reflection: A Social-Cognitive Analysis of Life Review. Review of
        General Psychology 5(2):148–60.
Stuttgen, Joanne Raetz
  1992 Enlarging Life Through Miniatures: Bill Austin's Roadside Carnival.
        Western Folklore 51(3-4):303–15.
Teske, Robert T.
  1985 State Folk Art Exhibitions: Review and Preview. *In* The Conservation of
        Culture: Folklorists and the Public Sector. Burt Feintuch, ed. Pp. 109–17.
        Lexington: University Press of Kentucky.
Titon, Jeff Todd
  1980 The Life Story. Journal of American Folklore 93(369):276–92.

Turner, Victor W.
    1969   Ritual Process: Structure and Anti-Structure. Chicago: Aldine Publishing
            Company.
Van Gennep, Arnold
    1960   [1909] The Rites of Passage. Michaela Visedom and Mari Caffee, trans.
            Chicago: University of Chicago Press.
Vlach, John Michael
    1988   Plain Painters: Making Sense of American Folk Art. Washington:
            Smithsonian Institution Press.
Vlach, John Michael and Simon J. Bronner, eds.
    1992   Folk Art and Art Worlds. Logan: Utah State University Press.
Wallace Brandon
    1992   Reconsidering the Life Review: The Social Construction of Talk about the
            Past, The Gerontologist 31(1):120–25.
Weatherford, Claudine
    1986   The Art of Queena Stovall: Images of Country Life. Ann Arbor, MI: UMI
            Research Press.
Webster, Jeffrey Dean, Ernst T. Bohlmeijer and Gerben J. Westerhof
    2010   Mapping the Future of Reminiscence: A Conceptual Guide for Research and
            Practice. Research on Aging. 32(4):527–64.
Werch-Takes, Joanna
    N.d.   "Arkansas Traveler: Work of an Itinerant Carver" at http://www.
            woodworking.com/ww/Article/Arkansas-Traveler-Work-of-an-Itinerant-
            Carver-8482.aspx, accessed September 9, 2014.
WFYI Media
    2006   Lest We Forget: A Survivor's Tale. DVD. Indianapolis, IN: WFYI Media
Yocom, Margaret R.
    1984   A Past Created for the Present: Selectivity and the Folk Paintings of Jessie
            Rhoads. A Review Essay. Kentucky Folklore Record 30(1):34–46.
Yocom, Margaret R., ed.
    1994   Logging in the Maine Woods: The Paintings of Alden Grant. Rangeley, ME:
            Rangeley Lakes Region Logging Museum.

Index

Some terms central to this work are too ubiquitous to meaningfully index. These include: aging, auto-biography, folk art, personal history, life-story objects.

JON KAY is professor of practice in Indiana University's Department of Folklore and Ethnomusicology. He directs Traditional Arts Indiana, the official statewide folk-arts program, which was recognized with a 2013 Governor's Arts Award for its work in documenting and promoting Indiana's traditional arts. He serves as the curator of folklife and cultural heritage at the Mathers Museum of World Cultures, where he conducts research, presents public programs, and produces exhibitions. Kay lectures on a wide range of topics related to folk art and material culture and hosts the periodic podcast *Artisan Ancestors*, which explores ways to research and understand the creative lives of people from the past.

CPSIA information can be obtained
at www.ICGtesting.com
Printed in the USA
LVOW06*1417220317

528096LV00019B/312/P

9 780253 022066